AllanBake

Really Good Cheesecakes

AllanBakes

Really Good Cheesecakes

with tips and tricks for successful baking

Allan Albert Teoh

mc Marshall Cavendish
Cuisine

The publisher wishes to thank Lian Yick Metal Tents Pte Ltd and Bai-Quo Pte Ltd for their support.

Editor : Lydia Leong
Designer : Bernard Go Kwang Meng
Photographer : Liu Hongde, Hongde Photography

Copyright © 2013 Marshall Cavendish International (Asia) Private Limited

Published by Marshall Cavendish Cuisine
An imprint of Marshall Cavendish International

Other Marshall Cavendish Offices:
Marshall Cavendish Corporation. 99 White Plains Road, Tarrytown NY 10591-9001, USA •
Marshall Cavendish International (Thailand) Co Ltd. 253 Asoke, 12th Floor, Sukhumvit 21 Road, Klongtoey Nua, Wattana, Bangkok 10110, Thailand • Marshall Cavendish (Malaysia) Sdn Bhd, Times Subang, Lot 46, Subang Hi-Tech Industrial Park, Batu Tiga, 40000 Shah Alam, Selangor Darul Ehsan, Malaysia.

Marshall Cavendish is a trademark of Times Publishing Limited

National Library Board, Singapore Cataloguing-in-Publication Data

Teoh, Allan Albert.
AllanBakes really good cheesecakes : with tips and tricks for successful baking / Allan Albert Teoh. – Singapore : Marshall Cavendish Cuisine, c2013.
pages cm.
ISBN : 978-981-4408-12-7 (paperback)

1. Cheesecake   2. Baking   I. Title.

TX773
641.8653 – dc23   OCN851628991

Printed in Malaysia by Tien Wah Press Pte Ltd

Dedication

To my youngest sister, Guat Bee and her husband, Yew Choon, who have always been there for me with their continuous love and unwavering support.

Contents

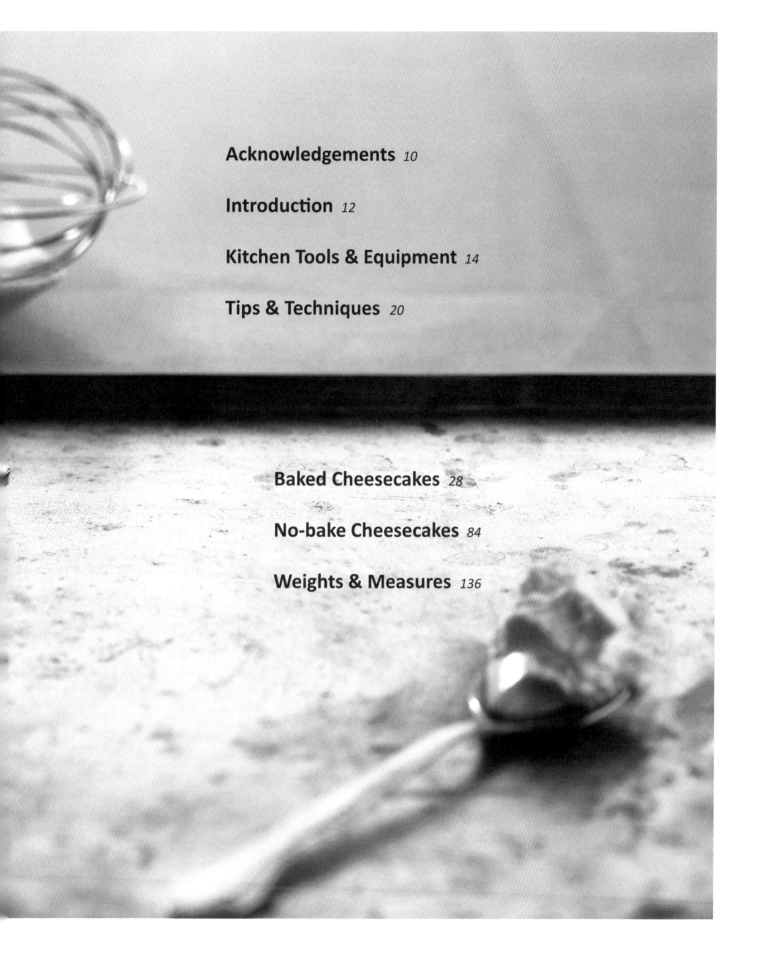

Acknowledgements

First and foremost, I would like to thank Lydia Leong for giving me the opportunity to do this third book, Bernard Go for his attention to detail and for making this book look its best, and the rest of the team from Marshall Cavendish International (Asia) Pte Ltd for testing and tasting all these cheesecakes. Your comments are invaluable to me and greatly appreciated.

My deepest appreciation also goes to:

The photographer, Liu Hongde, for making each photography session an adventure of food, laughter and fun.

Steven Lim and Shirley See for going beyond the call of friendship to sponsor the ingredients used for testing the recipes and the photography sessions. I'm fortunate to have friends like you. And to finally answer your question, "Yes, the cheesecake book is finally done!"

Vincent Pang for providing the fresh fruit for the recipes I created. Your patience and unwavering support has helped me translate my creations into this wonderful book.

And to those who helped me in one way or another at various points in my life:

Abigail Chay, thank you for your unflagging support, thoughtfulness and helpfulness.

Jeffrey Koh, your friendship in times of crisis has enabled me to keep myself firmly rooted in what I believe in.

James Koh and Helen Chong, thank you for your friendship over the years.

Richard Yeoh, your constant encouragement and moral support have helped me grow stronger.

Roselind Ng and Mabel Ng (of Forever Living Products) for making me look good in the pictures.

To my customers, friends and fans from Australia, China, Hong Kong, India, Indonesia, Japan, Korea, Malaysia, New Zealand, Pakistan, Philippines, Thailand, Taiwan, USA and UK. You believe in me and share my passion. For that, I am forever grateful.

My siblings, thank you for quietly supporting me in all I do even if it did not seem promising at times. (Thanks Guat Bee for always being there. If we were to live life all over again, I would still like to be your brother and instead of having you look out for me, it would be my turn to take care of you.)

The Ganapathy and Chandiram families for treating me as family. Thank you for your love.

Introduction

When I first started baking, the very first cake I put together was a cheesecake. When I opened my café and bake shop, I specialised in making cheesecakes. Throughout these years, many of the accolades and awards I have received were also about my cheesecakes. And all this time, customers and friends have always asked when I would put together a collection of cheesecake recipes. So here it is! My recipes to success—cheesecakes!

Cheesecakes have wonderfully rich and creamy fillings and equally delicious bases or crusts to compliment the fillings. It's hard to go wrong with cheesecakes when you're serving them at parties or giving them to friends.

In this book, I have included recipes for baked and no-bake cheesecakes comprising traditional favourites as well as new creations with a variety of bases. There are also a handful of lighter options for indulgence with less of the guilt! Most are simple to do, but most importantly, all can be prepared in advance so you can sit back, relax and enjoy your cake!

I have carefully worded the recipes to provide the necessary guidance for you to put these cheesecakes together. I sincerely hope that you will be able to use this book to create lovely cheesecakes whatever the occasion!

Enjoy!

Kitchen Tools and Equipment

Baking Pans

In this book, the size and shape of the baking pans used are specified to ensure the best results. Should you wish to make substitutions, do be aware that the results may vary.

Invest in good quality pans that do not scorch and distort. For baking cheesecakes, use a baking pan with a removable base or a springform pan with a removable base which will allow the cheesecake to be removed easily. When using such pans in a water bath, wrap the outside of the pan well with aluminium foil to prevent water seeping into the pan.

Pans and tins with a non-stick coating will also make it easier for the cheesecake to be removed. Be careful not to cut or scrape the pans and tins with sharp instruments to avoid scraping off the coating.

You may also use disposable aluminium trays for baking or setting cheesecakes in, as the tray can be cut away to release the cake.

Roasting pans used for baking cheesecakes are usually deep for the purpose of holding water for baking the cheesecakes in a water bath. The pan should also be wide enough for holding the cheesecake pan. Deep baking pans can also be used for the same purpose.

Food Processor

A food processor is useful to have in any kitchen and it will come in handy for making cheesecakes as well. Some manufacturers have created equipment that come with multiple attachments for juicing, puréeing, chopping and grating. Choose one that is most appropriate for your needs.

Grater

Available in various forms, as a flat grater or box grater, this handheld kitchen utensil allows you to grate or shred ingredients into coarse, medium or fine pieces. Grater-zesters are also available which allow you to grate citrus zest and chocolate into extra fine pieces.

Kitchen Scale

Accurate measuring of ingredients is essential for success when baking cheesecakes, so invest in a good quality kitchen scale. If possible, get a digital kitchen scale as it would offer more precise measurements, especially when working with small quantities. Always place the empty container on the scale, then set the scale to zero before placing the ingredients in to be weighed. Although dry measuring cups are available for measuring dry ingredients, a kitchen scale would offer more accuracy.

Knives

There are two kinds of knives used for cutting cakes, those with serrated edges and those with non-serrated edges. Knives with serrated edges are commonly used for cutting cakes with light textures while non-serrated knives are used for cutting denser cakes such as cheesecakes.

A small sharp knife is useful for unmoulding cheesecakes. Run the knife around the edge of the mould, pressing it against the side of the mould to release the cake.

Measuring Cups

In the kitchen, liquids are typically measured using liquid measuring cups. You may want to invest in a heatproof measuring cup so it can be used with hot liquids as well. When using liquid measuring cups, place the cup on a flat surface and pour in the liquid until it reaches the desired mark/level. It is important that you take the reading at eye level to ensure accuracy.

Measuring Spoons

Measuring spoons are useful for measuring small quantities of ingredients such as baking powder, salt, orange zest and essences. Measuring spoons usually come in a set of six: $1/8$ tsp, $1/4$ tsp, $1/2$ tsp, 1 tsp, $1/2$ Tbsp and 1 Tbsp. When measuring dry ingredients, always level the ingredient with the blade of a knife.

Mixer (Handheld or Stand Mixer)

If you're serious about baking, an electric mixer is an essential tool to own as it saves both time and effort. A heavy-duty stand mixer with different attachments such as a balloon whisk and paddle will help with whisking and beating. Handheld mixers are not as sturdy as stand mixers, but they are great for small jobs like mixing and whipping ingredients that require being heated in a water bath or on a stove. There are many brands of mixers available and different brands mean different speeds, so get to know your own mixer.

Mixing Bowls

It is useful to have different sizes of mixing bowls on hand. Having the right size of bowl for a particular recipe is important as it will help reduce the time needed to mix, beat or whisk the mixture. Mixing bowls can be made of plastic, glass or stainless steel. Of these three types, stainless steel is the easiest to clean and is most suitable when whisking egg whites where a grease-free and chilled bowl will yield the best results.

Oven Thermometer

Ovens are rarely accurate unless they are new or regularly calibrated and an oven that is too hot or not hot enough can affect the outcome of your cake. An oven thermometer will help you know the real temperature of your oven to avoid an overbaked or under-baked cake! A range of oven thermometers is available. Find one that suits your budget and your requirements. I use a dial thermometer with large print as it is easy to use and read.

Piping Bags and Piping Tips

Also known as pastry bags and pastry tips, these baking tools are readily available from baking supply stores. You can choose between reusable and disposable piping bags, but disposable piping bags make cleaning up less of a hassle. There are many different types of piping tips available, from plain round to star and flower tips, in various sizes. Have fun experimenting with the different tips. There's really no limit to how creative you can get!

Rolling Pin

Rolling pins come with or without handles and can be made of wood or metal. Rolling pins are useful for rolling out dough as well as for crushing biscuits for cake bases.

Sieve/Sifter

These are used for aerating and combining dry ingredients. Sieves can be made of plastic or metal and can come with or without handles. A simple bowl-shaped sieve with a fine wire mesh will work fine. It would be handy to have 2 or 3 sieves of different sizes on hand for different purposes. While a large or medium sieve will be useful for sifting large amounts of flour, a small sieve will be more suitable for sifting icing sugar, cocoa or green tea powder for decorating cakes.

Wire Cooling Rack

Cooling racks come in different sizes and shapes. It is good to have a few large rectangular ones that can accommodate a few batches of baked products. Wire racks aid cooling by allowing air to circulate on all sides of the baked product.

Wooden Spoons and Spatulas

Wooden spoons that come in various shapes and sizes are always good to have on hand. As they do not conduct heat, they are useful when handling heated mixtures. Such spoons will also not scrape and spoil the bottom of metal pans.

Spatulas are useful for scraping mixtures from mixing bowls and smoothening the tops of cakes prior to baking or setting. They are also useful for folding in beaten mixtures by hand without destroying their aeration.

Tips & Techniques

Equipment

Sealing Pans

When baking with springform pans or pans with a removable base, ensure that they are well sealed to prevent water leaking into the pan. To do this, wrap the outside of the pan with a large sheet of heavy-duty aluminium foil. The sheet of aluminium foil should be large enough to cover the base and sides of the pan completely. Wrap the pan with 2 or 3 layers of aluminium foil if desired.

Lining Pans

If using a baking pan without a removable base, line the pan with aluminium foil and leave an overhang to enable the cake to be lifted out of the pan easily once it is set. For no-bake cheesecakes, you can also use plastic wrap to line the pan.

Substituting Pans

If you intend to use a pan different from that specified in the recipes for baked cheesecakes, be aware that this may alter the surface area and depth of the cheesecake and hence affect the baking time and outcome of the cake. If you are intending to use a different pan, choose one that is closest in volume to the pan specified in the recipe to ensure that the baking time and temperature will not differ too much.

Ingredients

Using Fresh Ingredients

Always use fresh ingredients when baking to ensure the quality of the final product.

When citrus juices are called for in a recipe, extract them fresh from the fruit. Bottled juices may contain preservatives which will affect the taste of the final product.

A variety of fresh fruit are used in this book. Use fruit that are in season or be creative and substitute with a fruit that is close to what the recipe requires, such as fresh blackberries with fresh blueberries or fresh jackfruit with fresh cempedak.

Storing Dry Ingredients

Keep dry ingredients such as flour, sugar, cocoa powder and nuts in airtight containers and away from direct heat or sunlight. Or store them in the refrigerator to extend their shelf life.

Substituting Ingredients

Several varieties of cheese are used in these recipes: cream cheese, cottage cheese, ricotta cheese and mascarpone. I have suggested using full fat and reduced fat options in certain recipes to make them lower in fat. If you intend to make your own substitutions, be aware that this will affect the taste and texture of the final product.

Bringing to Room Temperature

Remove refrigerated ingredients such as cream cheese, butter, milk and eggs and leave them to sit at room temperature for about 20 minutes before using. When allowed to soften, block ingredients such as cream cheese and butter will be easier to beat, leading to greater aeration and a lighter final product. Milk and eggs at room temperature will also blend more easily, so the batter is not over beaten which could result in a dense product.

Using Gelatine

Gelatine is used in no-bake cheesecakes to give the cream cheese layer structure. To use, sprinkle the powdered gelatine into some water and leave for about 5 minutes for the gelatine to bloom. Add some hot water and stir until the gelatine is completely dissolved. Do not boil the mixture as the gelatine will become stringy and unusable. When incorporating the gelatine into the cream cheese mixture, check that both mixtures are around the same temperature as lumps may form if the gelatine mixture is too warm.

Using Eggs

In these recipes, large eggs weigh approximately 68 g and medium eggs weigh approximately 58 g.

When adding eggs into the cheese mixture, add them one by one and beat on low speed until just combined. Do not over beat as this may introduce too much air into the batter and cause the cheesecake to puff up while baking, then fall.

Techniques

Beating

When beating cream cheese using an electric mixer, use a paddle attachment and start at the lowest speed before gradually increasing to the speed recommended in the recipe. This will help stabilise the cheese and prevent it from splitting when other ingredients are added.

Avoid over beating the cream cheese as this may introduce too much air into the batter, leading the cheesecake to puff up during baking, then fall and crack.

Stop the mixer once or twice to scrape down the sides of the mixing bowl. This is to ensure that the ingredients are thoroughly mixed.

Preheating

Preheat the oven and bring it to the right temperature before putting the baking pan into the oven.

Baking

Release any air bubbles in the batter before baking. Do this by tapping the baking pan lightly on a solid surface, then using a small sharp knife to burst any bubbles that rise to the surface.

Bake cheesecakes on the lower middle rack of the oven.

The centre of the baked cheesecake will still be slightly wobbly after baking. It will set and firm up as it cools.

Do not remove cheesecakes from the oven immediately after baking. Leave the cheesecake to cool and set in the oven. It may take 1–2 hours for the cheesecake to cool completely.

Preventing Cracks

Baked cheesecakes may crack due to uneven heating and this is especially so with larger cakes. To prevent the top of your cheesecake from cracking, bake it in a water bath (bain marie). A water bath provides a moist environment and encourages the heat to be distributed more evenly in the oven. A water bath will also ensure that the baked cheesecake will have a creamier texture. To do this, fill a large pan with hot water until it reaches halfway up the sides of the baking pan. If baking in a shallow pan, place the pan on a wire rack so it sits above the water.

It is also important to grease the sides of the cake pan well so the sides of the cake do not stick to the pan while baking and lead to cracks.

When baking, do not open the oven door as the sudden draft of cool air will cause the top of the cake to shrink, leading to cracks on the surface.

If cracks do appear on your cheesecake after baking, don't fret. Just cover up the flaw with toppings such as whipped cream or fruit.

Baking Ahead

Different cake bases are used in the recipes in this book. If making a cake base using sponge cake, red velvet cake or carrot cake, these can be baked ahead to spread out the work.

Garnishing Cheesecakes

Always leave no-bake cheesecakes to set overnight in the refrigerator before garnishing. This will help minimise any flaws in the final product. When the cake has had sufficient time to set and gel properly, you can garnish it without having to worry about fruit juices or other liquids flowing into the cream cheese layer and spoiling the look of the cake.

Unmoulding Cheesecakes

To unmould cheesecakes, run a small sharp knife around the sides of the pan to loosen the cake. Remove the cake ring, then gently insert a long palette knife under the cake to ease it from the base plate.

Cutting Cheesecakes

Cutting cheesecakes neatly and cleanly can be a whizz when you know how! Run a long sharp knife over a naked flame to heat it, then make a single cut in the cake. Wipe it clean and repeat to heat the knife and make another cut until the desired pieces are obtained.

Storing Cheesecakes

To store cheesecakes, wrap them well with aluminium foil. Cheesecakes will keep refrigerated for up to 4 days.

Baked cheesecakes can also be kept in the freezer for up to 3 weeks. Bring to room temperature before serving.

Baked Cheesecakes

No-frills Old-fashioned Cheesecake

Makes one 23-cm round cake

DIGESTIVE BISCUIT BASE

Digestive biscuits *200 g*

Unsalted butter *180 g, melted*

Palm sugar (gula melaka) *1 Tbsp, melted*

FILLING

60% less fat cream cheese *330 g*

Castor sugar *60 g + 1 Tbsp*

Vanilla extract *$1^1/_2$ tsp*

Lemon juice *2 tsp*

Finely grated lemon zest *1 tsp*

Cornflour *$1^1/_2$ Tbsp*

Egg yolks *2, medium*

Double cream (48% fat) *80 ml*

Egg whites *2, medium*

Unsalted butter *1 Tbsp, melted*

- Grease a 23-cm round springform pan and wrap the outside of pan with aluminium foil. Preheat oven to 160°C.

- Prepare base. Place digestive biscuits in a food processor and process until fine. Transfer to a mixing bowl and add melted butter and palm sugar. Mix well. Press mixture evenly into the base and sides of prepared springform pan and bake for 15 minutes. Leave to cool, then freeze until ready to use.

- Keep oven heated at 160°C.

- Prepare filling. Using an electric mixer with a paddle attachment, beat cream cheese and 60 g sugar at medium speed until smooth. Add vanilla extract, lemon juice, lemon zest and cornflour and beat until incorporated. Add egg yolks, one at a time, beating for 20 seconds after each addition. Add double cream and mix well. Set aside.

NOTE:

To add another dimension to this recipe, add 3–4 Tbsp chocolate chips, sultanas or raisins to the filling before folding in the egg whites.

- In another mixing bowl with a whisk attachment, whisk egg whites at low speed until foamy. Add 1 Tbsp sugar, then increase speed to medium and whisk until stiff peaks form. Using a metal spatula, fold egg white meringue into cream cheese mixture.

- Pour filling over prepared base and bake for 1 hour. Lower oven temperature to 150°C and bake for another 20 minutes.

- Turn oven off and leave cake to cool in oven for 1 hour with oven door ajar. When cool, remove cake from oven and run a small knife around the side of pan to loosen cake. Do not unclip pan. Remove aluminium foil and refrigerate overnight.

- To unmould cake, run a small knife around the side of pan. Release clip and lift cake out of ring. Insert a palette knife under the base of cake and lift cake onto a serving plate.

- Garnish as desired and serve chilled.

Lemon Cheesecake with Lemon Mousse Topping

Makes one 23-cm round cake

COCONUT-ALMOND BASE

Desiccated coconut *60 g*

Ground almonds *120 g*

Plain (all-purpose) flour *120 g, sifted*

Dark brown sugar *60 g*

Unsalted butter *250 g, melted*

FILLING

Cream cheese *600 g, at room temperature*

Castor sugar *180 g*

Milk *100 ml*

Plain (all-purpose) flour *3 Tbsp*

Vanilla extract *1 Tbsp*

Salt *1/4 tsp*

Lemon *1, grated for zest and squeezed for juice*

Sour cream *150 ml*

Eggs *3, medium, at room temperature*

Egg yolk *1, medium, at room temperature*

MOUSSE

Whipping cream (35% fat) *100 ml , chilled*

Cream cheese *125 g*

Plain yoghurt *60 g*

Castor sugar *70 g*

Lemon *1, grated for zest and squeezed for juice*

Lemon paste *1 Tbsp*

Crystallised ginger *1 Tbsp, cut into small pieces*

- Grease a 23-cm round springform pan and wrap the outside of pan with aluminium foil. Have ready a deep roasting pan large enough to hold springform pan. Preheat oven to 160°C.

- Prepare base. In a mixing bowl, combine desiccated coconut, ground almonds, flour and sugar. Mix well. Add melted butter and bring mixture together. Press mixture evenly into the base and sides of prepared springform pan and bake for 20 minutes. Leave to cool, then freeze until ready to use.

- Keep oven heated at 160°C.

- Prepare filling. Using an electric mixer with a paddle attachment, beat cream cheese and sugar at medium speed until smooth. Add milk, flour, vanilla extract, salt, lemon juice and zest and mix until incorporated. Add sour cream and mix well. Reduce mixer speed and add eggs, one at a time, beating for 20 seconds after each addition.

- Pour filling over prepared base and place springform pan into roasting pan. Fill roasting pan with hot water until it reaches halfway up the side of springform pan. Bake for 1 hour, then lower oven temperature to 150°C and bake for another 30 minutes.

- Turn oven off and leave cake to cool in oven for 1 hour with oven door ajar. When cool, lift springform pan from water bath and remove foil. Run a small knife around the side of pan to loosen cake. Do not unclip pan. Refrigerate overnight.

- Prepare mousse. In another mixing bowl with a whisk attachment, whisk whipping cream at medium speed for 1–2 minutes until soft peaks form. Set aside.

- In a third mixing bowl with a clean paddle attachment, beat cream cheese and yoghurt at medium speed until smooth. Add castor sugar and lemon zest and mix well. Beat in lemon juice, lemon paste and crystallised ginger. Using a metal spatula, fold in whipped cream in 3 additions. Spoon mousse onto chilled cake, spreading it out with the back of a spoon. Refrigerate until ready to serve.

- To unmould cake, run a small knife around the side of pan. Release clip and lift cake out of ring. Insert a palette knife under the base of cake and lift cake onto a serving plate.

- Garnish as desired and serve chilled.

White Chocolate Honey Cheesecake with Dark Cookie Base

Makes one 23-cm round cake

DARK COOKIE BASE

Dark chocolate sandwich cookies *400 g*

Unsalted butter *250 g, melted*

FILLING

Cream cheese *500 g, at room temperature*

Honey *6 Tbsp*

Finely grated lemon zest *1 tsp*

Lemon juice *1 tsp*

Milk *2 Tbsp*

Cornflour *2 Tbsp*

Sour cream *80 ml*

Eggs *2, medium*

Egg yolks *2, medium*

White chocolate *90 g, melted*

GARNISHING

White chocolate buttons *as desired*

Honey *as desired*

- Grease a 23-cm round springform pan and wrap the outside of the pan with aluminium foil.

- Prepare base. Place cookies in a food processor and process until fine. Transfer to a mixing bowl and add melted butter. Mix well. Press mixture evenly into the base and sides of prepared springform pan, then freeze until ready to use.

- Preheat oven to 160°C.

- Prepare filling. Using an electric mixer with a paddle attachment, beat cream cheese at medium speed until smooth. Add honey and beat again. Add lemon zest, lemon juice, milk, cornflour and sour cream and mix until incorporated. Reduce mixer speed and add eggs and egg yolks, one at a time, beating for 20 seconds after each addition. Stir in melted white chocolate.

- Pour filling over prepared base and bake for 1 hour 30 minutes.

- Turn oven off and leave cake to cool in oven for 1 hour with oven door ajar. When cool, remove cake from oven and run a small knife around the side of pan to loosen cake. Do not unclip pan. Remove aluminium foil and refrigerate overnight.

- To unmould cake, run a small knife around the side of pan. Release clip and lift cake out of ring. Insert a palette knife under the base of cake and lift cake onto a serving plate.

- Garnish with white chocolate buttons and drizzle with honey. Serve chilled.

Blackberry Honey Crumble Cheesecake with Sweet Shortcrust Base

Makes one 23-cm round cake

SWEET SHORTCRUST BASE

Plain (all-purpose) flour *250 g*

Golden castor sugar *70 g*

Finely grated lemon zest *2 tsp*

Unsalted butter *150 g, cubed*

Egg yolks *2, medium*

Vanilla extract *2 tsp*

Water *1 tsp*

FILLING

60% less fat cream cheese *400 g, at room temperature*

Castor sugar *170 g*

Salt *1/4 tsp*

Milk *5 Tbsp*

Vanilla extract *2 tsp*

Plain (all-purpose) flour *2 Tbsp*

Finely grated lemon zest *1 tsp*

Lemon juice *1 tsp*

Sour cream *120 ml*

Eggs *2, medium*

Egg yolk *1, medium*

Puréed blackberries *200 g*

Blackberries *200 g*

HONEY CRUMBLE

Plain (all-purpose) flour *80 g, sifted*

Light brown sugar *80 g*

Unsalted butter *3 Tbsp, melted*

Manuka honey *1 1/2 Tbsp*

- Prepare base. Sift flour 3 times, then place into a food processor with sugar and lemon zest. Pulse for a minute, add butter and pulse until a coarse meal is formed. Add 1 egg yolk, followed by 1 tsp vanilla extract and process. Repeat with remaining egg yolk and vanilla extract and process until a dough is formed. If mixture doesn't bind, add a little water to help bring it together. Cover dough with plastic wrap and refrigerate for about 1 hour.

- Grease a 23-cm round springform pan and wrap the outside of pan with aluminium foil. Have ready a deep roasting pan large enough to hold springform pan.

- Place chilled dough between 2 sheets of plastic wrap and using a rolling pin, roll dough into 5-mm thick sheet. Press dough onto the base and sides of prepared springform pan. Using a fork, prick dough. Refrigerate for 30 minutes.

- Preheat oven to 180°C. Bake chilled base for 15–20 minutes until golden brown. Set aside to cool.

- Lower oven temperature to 160°C.

- Prepare filling. Using an electric mixer with a paddle attachment, beat cream cheese and sugar at medium speed until smooth. Add salt, milk, vanilla extract, flour, lemon zest and lemon juice and mix well. Add sour cream and beat for 1 minute. Reduce mixer speed and add eggs and egg yolk, one at a time, beating for 20 seconds after each addition.

- Divide filling into 2 portions. Add puréed blackberries to one portion and add whole blackberries to the other. Pour puréed blackberry filling over prepared base and place springform pan into roasting pan. Fill roasting pan with hot water until it reaches halfway up the side of springform pan. Bake for 30 minutes, then top with remaining filling and bake for 1 hour.

- Turn oven off and leave cake to cool in oven for 1 hour with oven door ajar. When cool, lift springform pan from water bath and remove foil. Run a small knife around the side of pan to loosen cake. Do not unclip pan. Refrigerate overnight.

- Prepare honey crumble. Preheat oven to 160°C. Mix flour and sugar. Add melted butter and honey and mix well. Spread mixture out on a baking tray and bake for 15–20 minutes until golden. Break up any large pieces of crumble with a fork. Set aside to cool.

- To unmould cake, run a small knife around the side of pan. Release clip and lift cake out of ring. Insert a palette knife under the base of cake and lift cake onto a serving plate.

- Garnish with honey crumble. Serve chilled.

Rose-flavoured Cheesecake with Almond Base

Makes one 23-cm round cake

ALMOND BASE

Ground almonds *220 g*

Icing sugar *120 g*

Unsalted butter *125 g, melted*

FILLING

Cream cheese *600 g, at room temperature*

Rose-flavoured sugar (see Note) *180 g*

Eggs *2, large*

Egg yolk *1, large*

Whipping cream (35% fat) *100 ml, chilled*

Cornflour *2 Tbsp*

Vanilla bean *1, split lengthwise, seeds scraped*

Rose water *1 Tbsp*

Orange juice *2 Tbsp*

Sour cream *125 ml*

- Grease a 23-cm round springform pan and wrap the outside of pan with aluminium foil. Have ready a deep roasting pan large enough to hold springform pan. Preheat oven to 180°C.

- Prepare base. In a mixing bowl, mix ground almonds and icing sugar. Add melted butter and mix until mixture resembles moist sand. Press mixture into the base and three-quarters up the sides of prepared springform pan. Bake for 15–20 minutes until golden brown. Leave to cool, then freeze until ready to use.

- Lower oven temperature to 160°C.

- Prepare filling. Using an electric mixer with a paddle attachment, beat cream cheese and sugar at medium speed until smooth. Reduce mixer speed and add eggs and egg yolk, one at a time, beating for 20 seconds after each addition. Add whipping cream, cornflour, vanilla seeds, rose water and orange juice and mix well. Add sour cream and beat until combined.

- Pour filling over prepared base and place springform pan into roasting pan. Fill roasting pan with hot water until it reaches halfway up the side of springform pan. Bake for 1 hour 20 minutes.

- Turn oven off and leave cake to cool in oven for 1 hour with oven door ajar. When cool, lift springform pan from water bath and remove foil. Run a small knife around the side of pan to loosen cake. Do not unclip pan. Refrigerate overnight.

- To unmould cake, run a small knife around the side of pan. Release clip and lift cake out of ring. Insert a palette knife under the base of cake and lift cake onto a serving plate.

- Garnish as desired and serve chilled.

NOTE:

Prepare rose-flavoured sugar at least a week ahead for the flavour to develop. Place 200 g dried rose buds and 100 g castor sugar into a blender and pulse until combined. Store in an airtight jar.

Peach and Orange Cheesecake with Sponge Cake Base

Makes two 20.5-cm square cakes

SPONGE CAKE BASE

Self-raising flour *80 g*

Salt *1/4 tsp*

Egg yolks *3, medium*

Corn oil *60 ml*

Milk *3 Tbsp*

Castor sugar *50 g + 50 g*

Vanilla extract *1 1/2 tsp*

Egg whites *3, medium, at room temperature*

Cream of tartar *1/2 tsp*

FILLING

Cream cheese *400 g, at room temperature*

Mascarpone cheese *120 g*

Plain yoghurt *100 g*

Icing sugar *200 g*

Orange juice *2 tsp*

Finely grated orange zest *1 tsp*

Vanilla extract *2 tsp*

Cornflour *2 Tbsp*

Egg yolks *2, large*

Canned peach halves *2 halves, puréed*

Egg whites *2, large*

- Grease two 20.5-cm square disposable aluminium cake pans. Have ready a deep roasting pan large enough to hold cake pans. Preheat oven to 170°C.

- Prepare base. Sift flour and salt together 3 times. Set aside. Using an electric mixer with a paddle attachment, beat egg yolks, oil, milk, flour mixture, 50 g sugar and vanilla extract at medium speed until well incorporated. Set aside.

- In another mixing bowl with a whisk attachment, whisk egg whites at medium speed for 1 minute. Add cream of tartar and remaining 50 g sugar and whisk at high speed until stiff peaks form.

- Fold half the egg white meringue into egg yolk mixture until well mixed, then fold in the rest of the egg white meringue.

- Pour batter equally into prepared cake pans and bake for 25–30 minutes or until a skewer inserted into the centre of cakes comes out clean. Leave to cool completely on a wire rack.

- Lower oven temperature to 160°C.

- Prepare filling. In a third mixing bowl with a clean paddle attachment, beat cream cheese, mascarpone cheese, yoghurt, icing sugar, orange juice and zest, vanilla extract and cornflour at medium speed until well mixed. Reduce mixer speed and add egg yolks, one at a time and beat for 20 seconds after each addition. Add puréed peaches and mix well.

- In a fourth mixing bowl with a clean whisk attachment, whisk egg whites at medium speed until soft peaks form. Fold egg white meringue into cream cheese mixture.

- Pour filling equally over cooled cake bases and place cake pans into roasting pan. Fill roasting pan with hot water until it reaches halfway up the side of cake pans. Bake for 1 hour 30 minutes.

- Turn off oven and leave cakes to cool in oven for 1 hour with oven door ajar. When cool, lift cake pans from water bath and refrigerate overnight.

- To unmould cakes, use a pair of scissors to cut open cake pans. Insert a palette knife under the base of cakes and lift onto a serving plate.

- Garnish as desired and serve chilled.

Chocolate Hazelnut Cheesecake with Cornflake Base

Makes 15 small cakes

CORNFLAKE BASE

Cornflakes *450 g, finely crushed*
Unsalted butter *250 g, melted*

FILLING

Cream cheese *500 g, at room temperature*
Light muscovado sugar *150 g*
Vanilla extract *2 tsp*
Eggs *3, medium*
Whipping cream (35% fat) *100 ml, chilled*

Cornflour *3 Tbsp*
Sour cream *150 ml*
Dark chocolate (70% cocoa) *150 g, melted*
Hazelnuts *150 g, finely ground*
Bailey's Irish cream (optional) *3 Tbsp*

GARNISHING (OPTIONAL)

Whipping cream (35% fat) *100 ml, chilled*
Icing sugar *1 Tbsp + more for dusting*
Cocoa powder *2 Tbsp*
Hazelnuts *15*

- Prepare 15 waxed paper muffin cups, each 7-cm wide. Have ready a shallow baking tray large enough to hold muffin cups, a deep roasting pan and a wire rack.

- Prepare base. Mix crushed cornflakes with melted butter. Press 1¹/₂ Tbsp mixture evenly into each muffin cup. Refrigerate for about 30 minutes.

- Preheat oven to 180°C. Place muffin cups on shallow baking tray and bake for 15 minutes. Set aside to cool.

- Lower oven temperature to 160°C.

- Prepare filling. Using an electric mixer with a paddle attachment, beat cream cheese and sugar at medium speed until smooth. Add vanilla extract and beat again. Reduce mixer speed and add eggs, one at a time, beating for 20 seconds after each addition. Add whipping cream and cornflour and beat until well mixed. Add sour cream and melted chocolate and mix well. Add ground hazelnuts and Irish cream, if using, and mix well.

- Pour filling into muffin cups on shallow baking tray. Place wire rack in roasting pan and place into the oven. Fill roasting pan with hot water, then place shallow baking tray on wire rack. Bake for 45 minutes.

- Turn oven off and leave cakes to cool in oven for 1 hour with oven door ajar. When cool, remove muffin cups from oven and refrigerate overnight. Let cheesecakes stand at room temperature for 10 minutes before serving.

- Prepare garnishing if desired. In another mixing bowl with a whisk attachment, whisk whipping cream at medium speed until soft peaks form. Add 1 Tbsp icing sugar and whisk until well mixed. Spoon whipping cream into a piping bag and pipe cream on cheesecakes. Dust with cocoa powder and icing sugar. Top with a hazelnut.

- Serve chilled.

Coffee Yoghurt Cheesecake with Brownie Base

Makes two 23-cm square cakes

BROWNIE BASE

Plain (all-purpose) flour *80 g*

Cocoa powder *2 Tbsp*

Double-action baking powder *³/₄ tsp*

Unsalted butter *100 g*

Dark chocolate buttons (70% cocoa) *50 g*

Brewed coffee *2 Tbsp*

Vanilla extract *¹/₂ tsp*

Eggs *2, large*

Brown sugar *150 g*

FILLING

Instant coffee granules *3 Tbsp + more for garnishing*

Cinnamon sugar *¹/₂ tsp*

Warm water *4 Tbsp*

Cream cheese *550 g, at room temperature*

Castor sugar *200 g*

Plain yoghurt *100 g*

Salt *¹/₂ tsp*

Cornflour *3 Tbsp*

Vanilla extract *2 tsp*

Amaretto liqueur (optional) *3 Tbsp*

Eggs *2, medium*

Egg yolks *2, medium*

Light sour cream *200 ml*

- Line two 23-cm square springform pans with aluminium foil and grease well. Wrap the outside of pans with aluminium foil. Have ready a deep roasting pan large enough to hold springform pan. Preheat oven to 180°C.

- Prepare base. Sift flour, cocoa powder and baking powder together 3 times. Set aside. In a heatproof bowl set over a pot of simmering water, melt butter and chocolate buttons, stirring to mix well. Add brewed coffee and vanilla extract and mix well. Remove from heat and add eggs, one at a time, stirring until smooth. Add sugar and mix well. Add flour mixture and whisk to incorporate.

- Pour batter equally into prepared springform pans and bake for 20–25 minutes or until a skewer inserted into the centre of cakes comes out clean. Leave to cool on a wire rack.

- Lower oven temperature to 160°C.

- Prepare filling. Dissolve coffee granules and cinnamon sugar in warm water. Set aside. Using an electric mixer with a paddle attachment, beat cream cheese and sugar at medium speed until combined. Add yoghurt and mix well. Add salt, cornflour, vanilla extract and amaretto liqueur, if using, and mix until incorporated. Reduce mixer speed and add eggs and egg yolks, one at a time, beating for 20 seconds after each addition. Add sour cream and mix well. Add coffee mixture and mix until well blended.

- Pour filling equally over prepared cake bases and place springform pans into roasting pan. Fill roasting pan with hot water until it reaches halfway up the side of springform pans. Bake for 1 hour 15 minutes.

- Turn oven off and leave cakes to cool in oven for 1 hour with oven door ajar. When cool, lift springform pans from water bath and remove foil. Run a small knife around the side of each pan to loosen cake. Do not unclip pans. Refrigerate overnight.

- To unmould cake, run a small knife around the side of pan. Release clip and lift cake out of ring. Insert a palette knife under the base of cake and lift cake onto a serving plate. Repeat with other cake.

- Garnish as desired and serve chilled.

Baked Durian Cheesecake

Makes two 18-cm round cakes

Sponge cake base *1 quantity (page 40)*

FILLING

Cream cheese *350 g, at room temperature*

80% less fat cream cheese *300 g*

Castor sugar *160 g*

Whipping cream (35% fat) *100 ml, chilled*

Cornflour *4 Tbsp*

Vanilla extract *2 tsp*

Orange juice *4 tsp*

Eggs *3, medium*

Egg yolks *2, medium*

Durian flesh *300 g, puréed*

TOPPING

Whipping cream *100 ml, chilled*

Durian flesh *300 g*

- Line two 18-cm round springform pans with aluminium foil and grease well. Wrap the outside of pans with aluminium foil.

- Prepare batter for base according to instructions on page 40 and bake base in prepared springform pans.

- Prepare filling. Preheat oven to 160°C. Using an electric mixer with a paddle attachment, beat both types of cream cheese with sugar at medium speed until well combined. Add whipping cream, cornflour, vanilla extract and orange juice and beat until incorporated. Reduce mixer speed and add eggs and egg yolks, one at a time, beating for 20 seconds after each addition. Add durian purée and mix well. Pour batter equally over prepared cake bases and bake for 1 hour 30 minutes.

NOTE:

If durian is not in season, replace it with cempedak or jackfruit. As the purée is made from pure fruit, it will vary in thickness depending on the water content of the fruit. Should the purée be too thick, dilute it with a little fresh milk before mixing it into the batter.

- Turn oven off and leave cakes to cool in oven with oven door ajar. When completely cool, lift springform pans from water bath and remove foil. Refrigerate for at least 24 hours.

- Prepare topping. Using an electric mixer with a whisk attachment and a clean, chilled mixing bowl, whisk whipping cream at medium speed for 1–2 minutes until soft peaks form. Add durian flesh and mix well. Refrigerate until needed.

- To unmould cake, run a small knife around the side of pan. Release clip and lift cake out of ring. Insert a palette knife under the base of cake and lift cake onto a serving plate. Repeat with other cake.

- Spoon topping over cakes and spread with the back of a spoon. Serve chilled.

Pineapple Cheesecake with Macadamia Nut Base

Makes one 23-cm round cake

MACADAMIA NUT BASE
Digestive biscuits *220 g*

Macadamia nuts *80 g*

Castor sugar *1 Tbsp*

Unsalted butter *150 g, melted*

FILLING
Cream cheese *400 g, at room temperature*

Golden castor sugar *150 g*

Eggs *2, large*

Salt *a pinch*

Vanilla extract *2 tsp*

Lemon juice *1/2 tsp*

Milk *3 Tbsp, mixed with 3 Tbsp cornflour*

Thickened cream (35% fat) *80 ml*

Canned crushed pineapple *5 Tbsp, drained + more for garnishing if desired*

Unsalted butter *2 Tbsp, melted*

- Grease a 23-cm round springform pan and wrap the outside of the pan with aluminium foil. Have ready a deep roasting pan large enough to hold springform pan. Preheat oven to 180°C.

- Prepare base. Place digestive biscuits, macadamia nuts and sugar in a food processor and process until fine. Add melted butter and mix well. Press mixture into the base and sides of prepared springform pan and bake for 20 minutes. Leave to cool, then freeze until ready to use.

- Lower oven temperature to 160°C.

- Prepare filling. Using an electric mixer with a paddle attachment, beat cream cheese and sugar at medium speed until smooth. Reduce mixer speed and add eggs, one at a time, beating for 20 seconds after each addition. Add salt, vanilla extract, lemon juice, milk and cornflour mixture and mix well. Add thickened cream, crushed pineapple and butter and mix until incorporated.

- Pour filling over prepared base and place springform pan into roasting pan. Fill roasting pan with hot water until it reaches halfway up the side of springform pan. Bake for 1 hour, then lower oven temperature to 140°C and bake for another 30 minutes.

- Turn oven off and leave cake to cool in oven for 1 hour with oven door ajar. When cool, lift springform pan from water bath and remove foil. Run a small knife around the side of pan to loosen cake. Do not unclip pan. Refrigerate overnight.

- To unmould cake, run a small knife around the side of pan. Release clip and lift cake out of ring. Insert a palette knife under the base of cake and lift cake onto a serving plate.

- Garnish as desired and serve chilled.

Dragon Fruit Cheesecake with Gingersnap Cookie Base

Makes five 12.5-cm round cheesecakes

GINGERSNAP COOKIE BASE

Gingersnap cookies *250 g, finely crushed*
Unsalted butter *200 g, melted*

FILLING

Dragon fruit *4 Tbsp + 1/2 fruit, cut into cubes*
Castor sugar *1 Tbsp*
Cream cheese *600 g, at room temperature*
Icing sugar *160 g*

Rose water *3 tsp*
Vanilla extract *1 tsp*
Plain (all-purpose) flour *5 Tbsp*
Double cream (48% fat) *125 ml*
Eggs *2, large*
Egg yolks *2, large*

TOPPING

Dragon fruit *1/2, cut into cubes*
Maple syrup *to taste*

- Prepare 5 round disposable aluminium cake pans, each 12.5-cm wide. Have ready a shallow baking tray large enough to hold cake pans. Preheat oven to 160°C.

- Prepare base. In a mixing bowl, combine gingersnap cookies and melted butter. Mix well. Press mixture evenly into the base of cake pans and bake for 15 minutes. Leave to cool, then freeze until ready to use.

- Keep oven heated at 160°C.

- Prepare filling. Using a food processor, purée 4 Tbsp dragon fruit and castor sugar until smooth. Set aside. Using an electric mixer with a paddle attachment, beat cream cheese and icing sugar at medium speed until smooth. Add rose water, vanilla extract, flour and double cream and mix until well combined. Lower mixer speed and add eggs and egg yolks, one at a time, beating for 20 seconds after each addition.

- Scatter cubed dragon fruit over prepared cookie bases, then pour filling evenly over bases. Place cake pans into shallow baking tray and fill baking tray with hot water until it reaches halfway up the side of cake pans. Bake for 1 hour 15 minutes.

- Turn oven off and leave cakes to cool in oven for 1 hour with oven door ajar. When cool, lift cake pans from water bath and refrigerate overnight.

- To unmould cakes, use a pair of scissors to cut open cake pans. Insert a palette knife under the base of cakes and lift onto a serving plate.

- Top with cubes of dragon fruit and drizzle with maple syrup. Serve chilled.

Banana Chocolate Chip Cheesecake with Walnut Biscuit Base

Makes three 20 x 10.5-cm cakes

WALNUT BISCUIT BASE

Digestive biscuits *200 g, crushed*

Walnuts *80 g*

Unsalted butter *150 g, melted*

FILLING

Cream cheese *400 g, at room temperature*

60% less fat cream cheese *250 g*

Golden castor sugar *150 g*

Eggs *3, medium*

Salt *$\frac{1}{4}$ tsp*

Vanilla extract *1 tsp*

Ripe bananas *120 g, peeled and mashed*

Banana essence *a drop*

Lemon juice *1 tsp*

Sour cream *150 ml*

Chocolate chips *150 g*

- Prepare 3 disposable aluminium loaf pans, each 20 x 10.5-cm. Have ready a shallow baking tray large enough to hold loaf pans. Preheat oven to 160°C.

- Prepare base. Place digestive biscuits and walnuts in a food processor and process until fine. Transfer mixture to a mixing bowl. Add melted butter and mix well. Divide mixture equally among loaf pans and press evenly into base of pans. Bake for 15 minutes. Leave to cool, then freeze until ready to use.

- Keep oven heated at 160°C.

- Prepare filling. Using an electric mixer with a paddle attachment, beat both types of cream cheese and sugar at medium speed until smooth. Reduce mixer speed and add eggs, one at a time, beating for 20 seconds after each addition. Add salt, vanilla extract, mashed bananas, banana essence, lemon juice and sour cream and mix well. Fold in half the chocolate chips.

- Pour filling equally over prepared biscuit bases. Scatter remaining chocolate chips over filling. Place loaf pans on shallow baking tray and fill baking tray with hot water.

- Bake for 45 minutes, then lower oven temperature to 140°C and bake for another 20 minutes.

- Turn oven off and leave cakes to cool in oven for 1 hour with oven door ajar. When cool, lift loaf pans from water bath and refrigerate overnight.

- To unmould cakes, use a pair of scissors to cut open loaf pans. Insert a palette knife under the base of cakes and lift onto a serving plate.

- Garnish as desired and serve chilled.

Sweet Potato Cashew Nut Cheesecake

Makes one 23-cm round cake

GINGERSNAP COOKIE BASE

Gingersnap cookies *250 g, finely crushed*

Unsalted butter *150 g, melted*

TOPPING

Cashew nuts *150 g, roughly chopped*

Dark brown sugar *90 g*

Unsalted butter *60 g, melted*

Plain (all-purpose) flour *4 Tbsp*

SWEET POTATO PURÉE

Sweet potatoes *200 g, peeled*

Castor sugar *2 Tbsp*

Lemon juice *1 tsp*

Finely grated lemon zest *1 tsp*

Salt *$1/2$ tsp*

Water *as needed*

FILLING

Cream cheese *650 g, at room temperature*

Dark brown sugar *150 g*

Ground cinnamon *1 tsp*

Ground cloves *a pinch*

Orange juice *$2^1/2$ Tbsp*

Rose water *1 tsp*

Vanilla extract *2 tsp*

Eggs *2, medium*

Egg yolks *2, medium*

Thickened cream (35% fat) *60 ml*

Sour cream *150 ml*

- Grease a 23-cm round springform pan and wrap the outside of pan with aluminium foil. Have ready a deep roasting pan large enough to hold springform pan.

- Prepare base. In a mixing bowl, combine gingersnap cookies and melted butter. Mix well. Press mixture into the base of springform pan, then freeze for at least 30 minutes.

- Preheat oven to 170°C.

- Prepare topping. In a mixing bowl, combine all ingredients and mix well. Spread mixture out on a baking tray and bake for 15 minutes. Leave to cool before using.

- Prepare sweet potato purée. Place sweet potatoes into a large heavy-based saucepan with sugar, lemon juice, lemon zest and salt. Add enough water to cover sweet potatoes and bring to the boil. When water is boiling, lower heat and simmer for about 30 minutes or until sweet potatoes are tender. Drain sweet potatoes and place into a food processor. Add 3–4 Tbsp liquid from saucepan and process until smooth. Refrigerate to chill purée before using.

- Preheat oven to 160°C.

- Prepare filling. Using an electric mixer with a paddle attachment, beat cream cheese and sugar at medium speed until smooth. Add chilled sweet potato purée, ground cinnamon, ground cloves, orange juice, rose water and vanilla extract and mix well. Reduce mixer speed and add eggs and egg yolks, one at a time, beating for 20 seconds after each addition. Add thickened cream and sour cream and beat until smooth.

- Pour filling over prepared base and place springform pan into roasting pan. Fill roasting pan with hot water until it reaches halfway up the side of springform pan. Bake for 1 hour, then lower oven temperature to 150°C. Sprinkle topping over filling, then bake for another 30–35 minutes or until centre is just set.

- Turn oven off and leave cake to cool in oven with oven door ajar. When completely cool, lift springform pan from water bath and remove foil. Run a small knife around the side of pan to loosen cake. Do not unclip pan. Refrigerate overnight.

- To unmould cake, run a small knife around the side of pan. Release clip and lift cake out of ring. Insert a palette knife under the base of cake and lift cake onto a serving plate. Serve chilled.

Calamansi White Chocolate Cheesecake with Pecan Base

Makes one 24 x 16-cm cake

PECAN BASE

Digestive biscuits *200 g, crushed*
Pecan nuts *80 g*
Unsalted butter *180 g, melted*

FILLING

Cream cheese *550 g, at room temperature*
Castor sugar *180 g*
Eggs *3, large*
Calamansi lime juice *3 Tbsp*
Vanilla extract *2 tsp*
Lime *1, grated for zest*
Light sour cream *150 ml*
Thickened cream (35% fat) *60 ml*
White chocolate buttons *150 g, melted*

- Line a 24 x 16-cm rectangular cake pan with aluminium foil, leaving an overhang for easy removal of cake. Grease well. Have ready a deep roasting pan large enough to hold cake pan. Preheat oven to 160°C.

- Prepare base. Place digestive biscuits and pecan nuts in a food processor and process until fine. Transfer mixture to a mixing bowl. Add melted butter and mix well. Press mixture evenly into base of cake pan and bake for 20 minutes. Leave to cool.

- Keep oven heated at 160°C.

- Prepare filling. Using an electric mixer with a paddle attachment, beat cream cheese and sugar at medium speed until smooth. Reduce mixer speed and add eggs, one at a time, beating for 20 seconds after each addition. Add calamansi juice, vanilla extract, lime zest, sour cream and thickened cream, mixing until incorporated. Add white chocolate and mix until combined.

- Pour filling over prepared pecan base and place cake pan into roasting pan. Fill roasting pan with hot water until it reaches halfway up the side of cake pan. Bake for 1 hour 20 minutes.

- Turn oven off and leave cake to cool in oven for 1 hour with oven door ajar. When cool, remove cake from oven and run a small knife around the side of pan to loosen cake. Refrigerate overnight.

- Lift cake out of pan using aluminium foil and place on a flat serving plate. Insert a palette knife under the base of cake and lift cake. Peel off aluminium foil and replace cake on serving plate.

- Garnish as desired and serve chilled.

Chocolate Lemon Grass Cheesecake

Makes six 250-ml jars

DIGESTIVE BISCUIT BASE

Digestive biscuits *180 g, finely crushed*

Unsalted butter *125 g, melted*

FILLING

Milk *200 ml*

Lemon grass *16 stalks; 4 coarsely chopped, 12 pounded and squeezed to obtain 2 tsp lemon grass extract*

Cocoa powder *2 Tbsp*

Chocolate emulco *1 Tbsp*

Warm water *3 Tbsp*

Cream cheese *675 g, at room temperature*

Sour cream *125 ml*

Light brown sugar *200 g*

Orange juice *2 Tbsp*

Vanilla extract *2 tsp*

Eggs *2, large*

Egg yolks *2, large*

Cornflour *3 Tbsp*

- Prepare six 250-ml wide mouth jars. Have ready a deep roasting pan large enough to hold jars.

- Prepare base. In a mixing bowl, combine digestive biscuits and melted butter. Mix well. Press 2–3 Tbsp mixture into the base of each jar, then freeze until ready to use.

- Preheat oven to 160°C.

- Prepare filling. In a heavy-based saucepan, heat milk and chopped lemon grass over medium heat, stirring until milk starts to bubble. Remove from heat and strain milk. Discard lemon grass. Measure out about 100 ml milk. Leave to cool.

- In a small bowl, mix cocoa powder, chocolate emulco and warm water into a paste. Set aside.

- Using an electric mixer with a paddle attachment, beat cream cheese, sour cream, sugar, orange juice and vanilla extract at medium speed until well mixed. Reduce mixer speed and add eggs and egg yolks, beating for 20 seconds after each addition. Add cornflour and mix well.

- Divide mixture into 2 portions. Add lemon grass milk and lemon grass extract to one portion and mix well. Add cocoa mixture to the other and mix well. Place tablespoonfuls of each filling alternately into prepared jars until filling is used up.

- Place jars in roasting pan and fill roasting pan with hot water until it reaches halfway up the side of jars. Bake for 1 hour.

- Turn oven off and leave cakes to cool in oven with oven door ajar. When cool, remove jars from water bath and refrigerate overnight.

- Garnish as desired and serve chilled.

Apple Cinnamon Cheesecake with Gingersnap Cookie Base

Makes 8 small cakes

Gingersnap cookie base *1 quantity (page 50)*

APPLE MIXTURE

Apples *3, medium, pared, cored and chopped*

Lemon juice *1 tsp*

Finely grated lemon zest *1 tsp*

Light brown sugar *3 Tbsp*

Ground cinnamon *1/2 tsp*

Ground cloves *a pinch*

Salt *a pinch*

Cornflour *1 Tbsp*

FILLING

60% less fat cream cheese *500 g, at room temperature*

Castor sugar *180 g*

Vanilla extract *1 1/2 tsp*

Lemon juice *1 Tbsp*

Ground cinnamon *1 tsp*

Salt *a pinch*

Cornflour *2 Tbsp*

Eggs *2, medium*

Egg yolks *2, medium*

Double cream (48% fat) *60 ml*

CARAMEL SAUCE (OPTIONAL)

Castor sugar *120 g*

Water *250 ml*

Pure cream (40% fat) *125 ml, warmed*

Butter *3 Tbsp, softened*

- Prepare 8 round disposable aluminium cake pans, each 10-cm wide. Have ready a deep roasting pan large enough to hold cake pans.

- Prepare base according to instructions on page 50 and bake base in prepared cake pans.

- Prepare apple mixture. Combine ingredients in a microwave-safe container and heat in the microwave oven on Medium for 6–8 minutes or until apples are soft. Mix well and leave to cool. Place cooled mixture into a food processor and pulse gently. Do not purée. Set aside.

- Preheat oven to 160°C.

- Prepare filling. Using an electric mixer with a paddle attachment, beat cream cheese and sugar at medium speed until smooth. Add vanilla extract, lemon juice, cinnamon, salt and cornflour and mix well. Reduce mixer speed and add eggs and egg yolks, one at a time, beating for 20 seconds after each addition. Add cream and mix well. Add apple mixture and incorporate.

- Pour filling equally over prepared cookie bases and place cake pans into roasting pan. Fill roasting pan with hot water until it reaches halfway up the side of cake pans. Bake for 1 hour 30 minutes.

- Turn oven off and leave cakes to cool completely in oven with oven door ajar. When cool, remove cakes from oven. Refrigerate overnight.

- Prepare caramel sauce if desired. Place sugar and water in a deep heavy-based saucepan. Stir over medium heat until sugar is dissolved. Increase to high heat and do not stir. Swirl pan to let mixture combine. Mixture will start to bubble. Let bubble for 5–6 minutes or until colour turns from light amber to reddish brown. Remove from heat. Mixture will start to smoke. Add warm cream while whisking. Mixture will bubble heavily. Add butter. Leave to cool completely before using.

- To unmould cakes, use a pair of scissors to cut open cake pans. Insert a palette knife under the base of cakes and lift onto a serving plate.

- Drizzle with caramel sauce and serve chilled.

Carrot Cake Cheesecake with Walnut Cream Cheese Frosting

Makes 25 small cakes

CARROT CAKE

Plain (all-purpose) flour *150 g*

Baking powder *¹/₂ tsp*

Bicarbonate of soda *¹/₂ tsp*

Ground cinnamon *1 tsp*

Light brown sugar *120 g*

Vanilla extract *¹/₂ tsp*

Corn oil *100 ml*

Eggs *2, large*

Salt *a pinch*

Carrots *150 g, peeled and grated*

Canned crushed pineapple *235 g, drained*

Desiccated coconut *2 Tbsp*

Sultanas *1¹/₂ Tbsp, soaked in warm water for 10 minutes, then drained*

CHEESECAKE

Cream cheese *350 g, at room temperature*

Sugar *90 g*

Vanilla extract *1 tsp*

Cornflour *1 Tbsp*

Eggs *2, medium*

Sour cream *4 Tbsp*

WALNUT CREAM CHEESE FROSTING

Cream cheese *500 g at room temperature*

Butter *200 g, softened*

Icing sugar *300 g, sifted*

Vanilla extract *2 tsp*

Lemon juice *2 tsp*

Walnuts *200 g, finely ground*

- Prepare 50 small muffin cups, each about 6.5-cm wide. Place 25 on a shallow baking tray and set the rest aside. Preheat oven to 170°C.

- Prepare carrot cake. Sift flour, baking powder, bicarbonate of soda and ground cinnamon together 3 times. Set aside. In a mixing bowl, combine sugar, vanilla extract, oil, eggs and salt with a wooden spoon. Add flour mixture and mix well. Stir in grated carrot, crushed pineapple, desiccated coconut and sultanas.

- Pour batter into prepared muffin cups and bake for 35–40 minutes or until a skewer inserted into centre of cakes comes out clean. Leave cakes to cool on a wire rack.

- Lower oven temperature to 160°C.

- Prepare cheesecake. Place remaining 25 muffin cups on a shallow baking tray. Using an electric mixer with a paddle attachment, beat cream cheese and sugar at medium speed until smooth. Add vanilla extract and cornflour and mix well. Reduce mixer speed and add eggs, one at a time, beating for 20 seconds after each addition. Add sour cream and mix thoroughly.

- Pour mixture into empty muffin cups until about one-third full and bake for 35–40 minutes.

- Turn oven off and leave cheesecakes to cool in oven for 1 hour with oven door ajar. Remove from oven and refrigerate overnight.

- Prepare frosting. Using an electric mixer with a paddle attachment, beat cream cheese until smooth. Add butter and beat until well mixed. Add icing sugar and beat to incorporate. Add vanilla extract, lemon juice and ground walnuts and mix well.

- To assemble, remove carrot cakes and cheesecakes from muffin cups. Slice carrot cakes horizontally in half. Place bottom halves on a wire rack and spread with a thin layer of frosting. Place a cheesecake on each frosted carrot cake. Top with more frosting and sandwich with other half of carrot cake. Cover with a thin layer of frosting.

- Garnish as desired and serve chilled.

Strawberry Stripe Cheesecake with Red Velvet Cake Base

Makes one 23-cm round cake

RED VELVET CAKE BASE

Cake flour *280 g*

Cocoa powder *2 Tbsp*

Salt *1/2 tsp*

Corn oil *180 ml*

Golden castor sugar *180 g*

Eggs *2, large*

Vanilla extract *1 tsp*

Red food colouring *2 tsp*

Buttermilk *250 ml*

Bicarbonate of soda *1 1/2 tsp*

White vinegar *1 tsp*

Lemon juice *1 tsp*

FILLING

Cream cheese *680 g, at room temperature*

Castor sugar *250 g*

Vanilla extract *3 tsp*

Orange juice *2 Tbsp*

Milk *4 Tbsp*

Plain (all-purpose) flour *4 Tbsp*

Sour cream *125 ml*

Eggs *4, medium*

Egg yolk *1, medium*

Strawberry purée *3 Tbsp*

Strawberry emulco *2 1/2 Tbsp*

- Grease a 23-cm round springform pan and wrap the outside of pan with aluminium foil. Have ready a deep roasting pan large enough to hold springform pan. Preheat oven to 180°C.

- Prepare base. Sift flour, cocoa powder and salt together 3 times. Set aside. Using an electric mixer with a paddle attachment, mix oil and sugar at medium speed. Reduce mixer speed and add eggs, one at a time, beating for 20 seconds after each addition. Add vanilla extract, red colouring and buttermilk. Mix well. Add flour mixture and incorporate. In a small bowl, combine bicarbonate of soda, vinegar and lemon juice. Add to batter and mix well.

- Pour batter into prepared springform pan and bake for 40 minutes or until a skewer inserted into the centre of cake comes out clean. Leave cake to cool.

- Preheat oven to 160°C.

- Prepare filling. Using an electric mixer with a paddle attachment, beat cream cheese and sugar at medium speed until smooth. Add vanilla extract, orange juice, milk, flour and sour cream and beat until well mixed. Reduce mixer speed and add eggs and egg yolk, one at a time, beating for 20 seconds after each addition.

- Divide filling into 2 portions. Add strawberry purée and emulco to one portion and beat until smooth. Leave the other portion plain.

- Using a ladle, spoon some plain filling onto the centre of prepared cake base. Using a clean ladle of the same size, spoon strawberry filling into the centre of plain filling. Repeat layering process until batter is used up. Do not tilt springform pan.

- Place springform pan into roasting pan and fill roasting pan with hot water until it reaches halfway up the side of springform pan. Bake for 1 hour 30 minutes.

- Turn oven off and leave cake to cool in oven for 1 hour with oven door ajar. When cool, lift springform pan from water bath and remove foil. Run a small knife around the side of pan to loosen cake. Do not unclip pan. Refrigerate overnight.

- To unmould cake, run a small knife around the side of pan. Release clip and lift cake out of ring. Insert a palette knife under the base of cake and lift cake onto a serving plate.

- Garnish as desired and serve chilled.

Avocado Ricotta Cheesecake with Coconut Sponge Cake Base

Makes one 23-cm square cake

COCONUT SPONGE CAKE BASE

Self-raising flour *80 g*

Egg yolks *3, medium*

Salt *1/4 tsp*

Corn oil *60 ml*

Castor sugar *50 g*

Coconut milk *3 Tbsp*

Milk *1 Tbsp.*

Egg whites *3, medium*

Cream of tartar *1/2 tsp*

Castor sugar *50 g*

FILLING

Cream cheese *450 g, at room temperature*

Ricotta cheese *120 g, at room temperature*

Castor sugar *180 g*

Avocado flesh *80 g, puréed*

Lemon juice *1 Tbsp*

Cornflour *4 Tbsp*

Rose water *1 tsp*

Vanilla extract *1 tsp*

Salt *a pinch*

Whipping cream (35% fat) *100 ml, chilled*

Eggs *4, medium, lightly beaten*

Avocado flesh *150 g, cut into cubes*

- Grease a 23-cm square springform pan and wrap the outside of pan with aluminium foil. Have ready a deep roasting pan large enough to hold springform pan. Preheat oven to 170°C.

- Prepare base. Sift flour 3 times. Set aside. Using an electric mixer with a paddle attachment, beat egg yolks, salt, oil, sugar, flour, coconut milk and milk at medium speed for 2 minutes. Set aside.

- In another mixing bowl with a whisk attachment, whisk egg whites at medium speed for 1 minute. Reduce mixer speed and add cream of tartar and sugar. Whisk for another 1 minute. Increase speed to high and whisk until stiff peaks form.

- Fold half the egg white meringue into egg yolk mixture until well mixed, then fold in the rest of the egg white meringue.

- Pour batter into prepared springform pan and bake for 40–45 minutes or until a skewer inserted into the centre of cake comes out clean. Set aside to cool.

- Keep oven heated at 170°C.

- Prepare filling. In a third mixing bowl with a clean paddle attachment, beat cream cheese, ricotta cheese and sugar at medium speed until smooth. Add puréed avocado, lemon juice, cornflour, rose water, vanilla extract, salt and whipping cream and beat until well incorporated. Reduce mixer speed and add lightly beaten eggs, a quarter at a time, beating for 20 seconds after each addition. Add cubed avocado and mix gently.

- Pour batter over prepared cake base and place springform pan into roasting pan. Fill roasting pan with hot water until it reaches halfway up the sides of springform pan. Bake for 1 hour 30 minutes.

- Turn oven off and leave cake to cool in oven for 1 hour with oven door ajar. When cool, lift springform pan from water bath and remove foil. Run a small knife around the side of pan to loosen cake. Do not unclip pan. Refrigerate overnight.

- To unmould cake, run a small knife around the side of pan. Release clip and lift cake out of ring. Insert a palette knife under the base of cake and lift cake onto a serving plate.

- Garnish as desired and serve chilled.

Liqueur Coffee Chocolate Swirl Cheesecake

Makes one 24-cm tart

DIGESTIVE BISCUIT BASE

Digestive biscuits *350 g, finely crushed*

Unsalted butter *200 g, melted*

FILLING

Dark chocolate buttons (70% cocoa) *50 g*

Instant coffee granules *2 tsp*

Warm water *1 Tbsp*

Irish cream liqueur or coffee-flavoured liqueur *2 Tbsp*

Cream cheese *280 g, at room temperature*

Golden castor sugar *70 g*

Light sour cream *2^1/$_2$ Tbsp*

Salt *a pinch*

Vanilla extract *1 tsp*

Plain (all-purpose) flour *1 Tbsp*

Egg *1, large*

Egg yolk *1, large*

- Grease a 24-cm round loose-bottom tart pan and wrap the outside of pan with aluminium foil. Have ready a shallow baking pan large enough to hold tart pan.

- Prepare base. In a mixing bowl, combine digestive biscuits and melted butter. Mix well. Press mixture into base and sides of tart pan, then freeze until ready to use.

- Prepare filling. Place chocolate buttons in a microwave-safe bowl and heat in the microwave oven on High for 30 seconds. Remove and stir. Repeat once or twice until chocolate is smooth. Be careful not to burn chocolate. Set aside to cool.

- Stir coffee granules into warm water. Add liqueur and mix well. Set aside.

- Using an electric mixer with a paddle attachment, beat cream cheese and sugar at medium speed until smooth. Add sour cream, salt, vanilla extract and flour and mix well. Reduce mixer speed and add egg and egg yolk, one at a time, beating for 20 seconds after each addition.

- Divide batter into 3 portions. Add melted chocolate to one portion and mix well. Add coffee mixture to another portion and mix well. Leave last portion plain.

- Spread some chocolate filling over prepared base, then top with half the coffee filling, pouring it in a circular motion, starting from the outside in. Pour half the plain filling over and repeat the layering process until filling is used up. Using a chopstick, gently swirl filling to create a marbled effect.

- Place tart pan into baking pan. Fill baking pan with hot water until it reaches halfway up the side of tart pan. Bake for 1 hour 15 minutes.

- Turn oven off and leave cake to cool in oven for 1 hour with oven door ajar. When cool, lift tart pan from water bath and remove foil. Refrigerate overnight or 24 hours if time permits.

- To unmould cake, gently push base plate up with your hands and remove ring. Insert a palette knife under the base of cake and lift cake onto a serving plate.

- Garnish as desired and serve chilled.

Mini Berry Cheesecake with Fruit Cake Base

Makes 8 small cakes

FRUIT CAKE BASE

Plain (all-purpose) flour *150 g*

Baking powder *¹/₂ tsp*

Bicarbonate of soda *¹/₂ tsp*

Mixed spices *¹/₂ tsp*

Ground cinnamon *¹/₂ tsp*

Vanilla powder *1 tsp*

Salt *¹/₂ tsp*

Dried mixed fruit *225 g*

Light brown sugar *110 g*

Unsalted butter *65 g*

Water *130 ml*

Orange essence *1 tsp*

Finely grated orange zest *¹/₂ tsp*

Eggs *2, medium*

FILLING

Light cream cheese *375 g, at room temperature*

Golden castor sugar *140 g*

Salt *a pinch*

Vanilla extract *1¹/₂ tsp*

Rose water *1 tsp*

Cornflour *1 Tbsp*

Light sour cream *100 ml*

Double cream (48% fat) *50 ml*

Eggs *2, large*

Unsalted butter *2 Tbsp, melted*

Mixed fresh berries *250 g*

- Grease 8 small springform pans (I used 10-cm heart-shaped pans) and wrap the outside of pans with aluminium foil. Have ready a deep roasting pan large enough to hold springform pans. Preheat oven to 180°C.

- Prepare base. In a mixing bowl, sift flour, baking powder, bicarbonate of soda, mixed spices, ground cinnamon, vanilla powder and salt together 3 times. Set aside.

- In a heavy-based saucepan over medium heat, boil mixed fruit, sugar, butter and water until bubbles appear. Remove from heat. Add orange essence and orange zest. Stir well and leave to cool on a wire rack.

- Using an electric mixer with a whisk attachment, whisk eggs at medium speed until foamy. Add to cooled fruit mixture and mix well. Fold in flour mixture in 3 additions until well mixed.

- Pour batter equally into prepared springform pans. Bake for 30 minutes or until cake is golden brown and has pulled away from the side of pan. Leave to cool completely on a wire rack.

- Keep oven heated at 160°C.

- Prepare filling. Using an electric mixer with a paddle attachment, beat cream cheese, sugar and salt at medium speed until smooth. Add vanilla extract and rose water and beat again. Add cornflour, sour cream and double cream and mix well. Reduce mixer speed and add eggs, one at a time, beating for 20 seconds after each addition. Add melted butter and mixed berries and beat until incorporated.

- Pour filling equally over prepared cake bases and place springform pans into roasting pan. Fill roasting pan with hot water until it reaches halfway up the sides of springform pans. Bake for 1 hour.

- Turn oven off and leave cakes to cool in oven for 1 hour with oven door ajar. When cool, lift springform pans from water bath and remove foil. Run a small knife around the side of each pan to loosen cakes. Do not unclip pans. Refrigerate for 24 hours.

- To unmould cake, run a small knife around the side of each pan. Release clip and lift cake out of ring. Insert a palette knife under the base of cake and lift cake onto a serving plate. Repeat with remaining cakes.

- Garnish as desired and serve chilled.

White Chocolate Peach Cheesecake

Makes two 36 x 13-cm cakes

DIGESTIVE BISCUIT BASE
Digestive biscuits *400 g, finely crushed*
Unsalted butter *250 g, melted*

FILLING
Cream cheese *500 g, at room temperature*
Castor sugar *140 g*
Salt *a pinch*
Vanilla extract *1 tsp*
Cornflour *2 Tbsp*
Light sour cream *130 ml*
Eggs *2, medium*
Egg yolks *2, medium*
White chocolate buttons *150 g, melted and cooled*
Canned peach halves *300 g, drained*

- Grease two 36 x 13-cm loose-bottom rectangular tart pans and wrap the outside of pans with aluminium foil. Have ready a shallow baking pan and a wire rack.

- Prepare base. In a mixing bowl, combine digestive biscuits and melted butter. Mix well. Press mixture into the base and sides of tart pans, then freeze until ready to use.

- Preheat oven to 160°C.

- Prepare filling. Using an electric mixer with a paddle attachment, beat cream cheese, sugar and salt at medium speed until smooth. Add vanilla extract, cornflour and sour cream and mix well. Reduce mixer speed and add eggs and egg yolks, one at a time, beating for 20 seconds after each addition. Add melted white chocolate and beat until completely mixed.

- Arrange peach halves on prepared biscuit bases and pour filling evenly over bases.

- Place wire rack in shallow baking pan and place into oven. Arrange tart pans on wire rack. Fill baking pan with hot water and bake for 1 hour.

- Turn off oven and leave cakes to cool in oven for 1 hour with oven door ajar. When cool, remove tart pans from oven and peel away foil. Refrigerate for 24 hours.

- To unmould cake, gently push base plate up with your hands and remove ring. Insert a palette knife under the base of cake and lift cake onto a serving plate. Repeat with other cake.

- Garnish as desired and serve chilled.

Orange and Red Date Cheesecake with Carrot Cake Base

Makes 24 small cakes

Carrot cake *1 quantity (page 62)*

FILLING

Cream cheese *600 g, at room temperature*

Golden castor sugar *160 g*

Vanilla extract *2 tsp*

Orange emulco *1 Tbsp*

Orange juice *2 Tbsp*

Finely grated orange zest *3 tsp*

Eggs *2, large*

Egg yolk *1, large*

Sour cream *80 ml*

Thickened cream (35% fat) *80 ml*

GARNISHING

Red dates *200 g, pitted and soaked with very hot water for 1 hour; reserve about 100 ml soaking liquid*

Whole red dates *24*

- Prepare two 12-hole muffin pans and line pans with paper muffin cups. Have ready a deep roasting pan large enough to hold muffin trays. Preheat oven to 170°C.

- Prepare batter for carrot cake according to instructions on page 62. Pour batter into prepared muffin pans and bake for 35–40 minutes or until a skewer inserted into centre of cakes comes out clean. Leave cakes to cool completely on a wire rack.

- Lower oven temperature to 160°C.

- Prepare filling. Using an electric mixer with a paddle attachment, beat cream cheese and sugar at medium speed until smooth. Add vanilla extract, orange emulco, orange juice and orange zest and mix well. Reduce mixer speed and add eggs and egg yolk, one at a time, beating for 20 seconds after each addition. Add sour cream and thickened cream and mix until well blended.

- Pour filling equally over prepared carrot cakes and place muffin pans into roasting pan. Fill roasting pan with hot water until it reaches halfway up the side of muffin pans. Bake for 1 hour 20 minutes.

- Turn oven off and leave cake to cool in oven for 1 hour with oven door ajar. When cool, lift muffin pans from water bath and refrigerate for 24 hours.

- Prepare garnishing. Process soaked red dates in a food processor, adding reserved soaking liquid by the teaspoon to help blades turn. Spoon red date purée into a piping bag and pipe onto cakes. Top with whole red dates.

- Serve chilled.

Chestnut Cheesecake with Butter Cookie Base

Makes two 20 x 10.5-cm cakes

BUTTER COOKIE BASE

Butter cookies *180 g, finely crushed*

Unsalted butter *150 g, melted*

FILLING

Pre-cooked chestnuts *240 g + 120 g*

Milk *2 Tbsp*

Cream cheese *500 g, at room temperature*

Castor sugar *180 g*

Eggs *3, medium*

Sour cream *150 ml*

Pure cream (40% fat) *4 Tbsp*

Vanilla extract *2 tsp*

Cornflour *3 Tbsp*

Orange juice *1 Tbsp*

- Prepare 2 disposable aluminium loaf pans, each 20 x 10.5-cm. Have ready a deep roasting pan large enough to hold loaf pans.

- Prepare base. In a mixing bowl, combine butter cookies and melted butter. Mix well. Press mixture evenly into base of loaf pans, then freeze until ready to use.

- Preheat oven to 160°C.

- Prepare filling. In a food processor, process 240 g chestnuts and milk into a purée. Set aside.

- Using an electric mixer with a paddle attachment, beat cream cheese and sugar at medium speed until smooth. Reduce mixer speed and add eggs, one at a time, beating for 20 seconds after each addition. Add sour cream, pure cream, vanilla extract, cornflour and orange juice and beat until incorporated. Add chestnut purée and mix well.

- Arrange remaining 120 g chestnuts on prepared cookie bases. Pour batter equally over and place loaf pans into roasting pan. Fill roasting pan with water until it reaches halfway up the sides of loaf pans. Bake for 1 hour 15 minutes.

- Turn oven off and leave cakes to cool completely in oven with oven door ajar. When cool, lift loaf pans from water bath and refrigerate overnight.

- To unmould cakes, use a pair of scissors to cut open loaf pans. Insert a palette knife under the base of cakes and lift onto a serving plate.

- Garnish as desired and serve chilled.

Pumpkin, Golden Raisin and Pistachio Cheesecake

Makes two 26 x 11.5-cm cakes

ALMOND BASE

Digestive biscuits 220 g, *finely crushed*

Ground almonds 100 g

Unsalted butter 180 g, *melted*

FILLING

Pumpkin 1, *small*

Cream cheese 500 g, *at room temperature*

Golden castor sugar 160 g

Rose water 2 tsp

Vanilla extract 2 tsp

Milk 60 ml

Plain (all-purpose) flour 4 Tbsp

Eggs 3, *large*

Light sour cream 180 ml

Shelled roasted pistachio nuts 100 g, *chopped*

Golden raisins 80 g, *chopped*

- Line two 26 x 11.5-cm loaf pans with aluminium foil, leaving an overhang for easy removal of cake. Grease well. Have ready a deep roasting pan large enough to hold loaf pans. Preheat oven to 180°C.

- Prepare base. In a mixing bowl, combine digestive biscuits and ground almonds. Add melted butter and mix well. Press mixture into the base and sides of loaf pans. Bake for 15 minutes. Leave to cool on a wire rack.

- Lower oven temperature to 160°C.

- Prepare filling. Cut pumpkin in half and scrape out seeds. Rinse. Place pumpkin halves face down on a lined baking tray. Bake for 1 hour 30 minutes–2 hours until pumpkin is tender and a skewer can be inserted easily. Remove from oven and let cool completely. Scrape flesh with a spoon and mash until smooth. Measure out 180 g mashed pumpkin for use in filling.

- Using an electric mixer with a paddle attachment, beat cream cheese and sugar at medium speed until smooth. Add rose water, vanilla extract, milk and flour and beat until incorporated. Reduce mixer speed and add eggs, one at a time, beating for 20 seconds after each addition. Beat in sour cream. Add mashed pumpkin, pistachios and raisins and mix well.

- Pour filling equally over prepared biscuit bases and place loaf pans into roasting pan. Fill roasting pan with hot water until it reaches halfway up the sides of loaf pans. Bake for 1 hour 25 minutes.

- Turn oven off and leave cakes to cool completely in oven with oven door ajar. When cool, lift loaf pans from water bath and refrigerate for 24 hours.

- Lift cakes out of pan using aluminium foil and place on a flat serving plate. Insert a palette knife under the base of cake and lift cake. Peel off aluminium foil and replace cake on serving plate.

- Garnish as desired and serve chilled.

Cottage Cheese, Berry and Chocolate Cheesecake with Carrot Cake Base

Makes 20–25 small cakes

Carrot cake *1 quantity (page 62)*

FILLING

Cream cheese *450 g, at room temperature*

Cottage cheese *130 g, at room temperature*

Golden castor sugar *160 g*

Vanilla extract *3 tsp*

Rose water *1$^{1}/_{2}$ tsp*

Orange juice *2 Tbsp*

Sour cream *160 ml*

Milk *3 Tbsp*

Plain (all-purpose) flour *2 Tbsp*

Eggs *2, large*

Egg yolk *1, large*

Frozen mixed berries *180 g, brought to room temperature before using*

Cocoa powder *1$^{1}/_{2}$ Tbsp*

Chocolate emulco *1 Tbsp*

Hot water *3–4 Tbsp*

- Prepare 20–25 waxed paper muffin cups, each 7-cm wide. Have ready a shallow baking tray large enough to hold muffin cups, a deep roasting pan and a wire rack. Preheat oven to 170°C.

- Prepare batter for carrot cake according to instructions on page 62 and pour batter into prepared muffin cups. Place muffin cups on a baking tray and bake for 35-40 minutes or until a skewer inserted into centre of cakes comes out clean. Leave muffin cups on tray.

- Lower oven temperature to 160°C.

- Prepare filling. Using an electric mixer with a paddle attachment, beat cream cheese, cottage cheese and sugar until smooth. Add vanilla extract, rose water, orange juice, sour cream, milk and flour and mix until incorporated. Reduce mixer speed and add eggs and egg yolk, one at a time, beating for 20 seconds after each addition.

- Spoon one-third of filling into another bowl. Add mixed berries and stir to mix. Set aside.

- In a small bowl, mix cocoa powder, chocolate emulco and enough hot water to get a paste. Add to remaining filling and mix well.

- Pour filling with berries equally over prepared carrot cakes, then pour chocolate filling over.

- Place wire rack in roasting pan and place into the oven. Fill roasting pan with hot water, then place shallow baking tray with muffin cups on wire rack. Bake for 1 hour 20 minutes.

- Turn oven off and leave cakes to cool in oven for 1 hour with oven door ajar. When cool, remove cakes and refrigerate for 24 hours.

- Garnish as desired and serve chilled.

Chocolate and Vanilla Cottage Cheese Cheesecake

Makes one 24-cm round cake

DIGESTIVE BISCUIT BASE

Digestive biscuits *180 g, finely crushed*

Unsalted butter *125 g, melted*

FILLING

Cream cheese *450 g , at room temperature*

Cottage cheese *150 g, at room temperature*

Golden castor sugar *180 g*

Sour cream *100 ml*

Pure cream (40% fat) *100 ml*

Vanilla extract *3 tsp*

Orange juice *3 Tbsp*

Milk *3 Tbsp*

Cornflour *2 Tbsp*

Eggs *2, large*

Egg yolks *2, large*

Cocoa powder *2 Tbsp*

Chocolate emulco *3 tsp*

Hot water *3–4 Tbsp*

- Grease a 24-cm round springform pan and wrap the outside of pan with aluminium foil. Have ready a deep roasting pan large enough to hold springform pan.

- Prepare base. In a mixing bowl, combine digestive biscuits and melted butter. Mix well. Press mixture into the base of springform pan, then freeze until ready to use.

- Preheat oven to 160°C.

- Prepare filling. Using an electric mixer with a paddle attachment, beat cream cheese, cottage cheese and sugar at medium speed until smooth. Add sour cream, pure cream, vanilla extract and orange juice and mix until incorporated. Add milk and cornflour and mix well. Reduce mixer speed and add eggs and egg yolks, one at a time, beating for 20 seconds after each addition. Pour half the filling into another bowl.

- In a small bowl, mix cocoa powder, chocolate emulco and enough hot water to get a paste. Add to one portion of filling and mix well.

- Pour one-third of plain filling onto prepared base, then top with one-third of chocolate filling. Repeat layering process until filling is used up. Using a skewer, create a pattern by drawing straight lines in filling starting from the centre and moving outwards.

- Place springform pan into roasting pan and fill roasting pan with hot water until it reaches halfway up the side of springform pan. Bake for 1 hour 30 minutes.

- Turn oven off and leave cake to cool in oven for 1 hour with oven door ajar. When cool, lift springform pan from water bath and remove foil. Run a small knife around the side of pan to loosen cake. Do not unclip pan. Refrigerate overnight.

- To unmould cake, run a small knife around the side of pan. Release clip and lift cake out of ring. Insert a palette knife under the base of cake and lift cake onto a serving plate.

- Garnish as desired and serve chilled.

No-bake
Cheesecakes

Mango Cheesecake with Pecan Base

Makes one 23-cm round cake

PECAN BASE

Digestive biscuits *130 g*

Pecans *60 g*

Castor sugar *2 Tbsp*

Unsalted butter *150 g, melted*

FILLING

Gelatine powder *1¹/₂ Tbsp*

Hot water *150 ml*

Cream cheese *300 g, at room temperature*

Castor sugar *5 Tbsp*

Orange juice *1 Tbsp*

Milk *150 ml*

Mango purée *250 g*

Mango *1, medium, peeled and cut into cubes*

- Grease a 23-cm round springform pan. Preheat oven to 160°C.

- Prepare base. Place digestive biscuits, pecans and sugar in a food processor and process until fine. Transfer mixture to a mixing bowl and add melted butter. Mix well. Press mixture evenly into the base of springform pan and bake for 15 minutes. Leave to cool, then freeze until ready to use.

- Prepare filling. Sprinkle gelatine powder over hot water and set aside for 5 minutes.

- Using a food processor, mix cream cheese, sugar, orange juice and milk until smooth. Add gelatine mixture and pulse for about 1 minute. Add mango purée and mix well.

- Pour filling over prepared base and scatter with cubed mangoes. Do not stir. Refrigerate overnight.

- To unmould cake, run a small knife around the side of pan. Release clip and lift cake out of ring. Insert a palette knife under the base of cake and lift cake onto a serving plate.

- Garnish as desired and serve chilled.

Lychee Konnyaku Cheesecake with Sweet Shortcrust Base

Makes one 23-cm round cake

Sweet shortcrust base *1 quantity (page 36)*

LYCHEE KONNYAKU

Canned lychees *2 cans, each 565 g*

Konnyaku jelly powder *10 g*

Icing sugar *120 g, sifted*

Water *1.1 litres*

Pandan leaves *3–4 stalks, bruised and knotted*

Red food colouring *a few drops*

FILLING

Gelatine powder *1^1/$_4$ Tbsp*

Hot water *120 ml*

Cream cheese *350 g, at room temperature*

Castor sugar *3^1/$_2$ Tbsp*

Honey *1 Tbsp*

Milk *120 ml*

Vanilla extract *2 tsp*

Whipping cream (35% fat) *150 ml chilled*

- Prepare base according to instructions on page 36.

- Prepare lychee konnyaku. Drain canned lychees and reserve 12 lychees for garnish. Purée rest of lychees and set aside.

- Mix jelly powder with icing sugar. Bring water to the boil with pandan leaves. When water is boiling, discard pandan leaves and lower heat to a simmer. Spoon some hot water into jelly powder mixture and stir until dissolved. Pour mixture into pot of boiling water and increase heat. Stir well.

- Spoon one-third of jelly mixture into a bowl and add a few drops of food colouring. Stir, then refrigerate to set. Add puréed lychees to remaining jelly mixture, stir well and remove from heat. Add a few drops of food colouring and pour mixture into a bowl. Refrigerate to set.

- Prepare filling. Sprinkle gelatine powder over hot water and set aside for 5 minutes. Using a food processor, process cream cheese, sugar, honey, milk and vanilla extract until combined. Add gelatine mixture and pulse until well incorporated.

- Using an electric mixer with a whisk attachment and a clean, chilled mixing bowl, whisk whipping cream at medium speed until medium peaks form. Using a metal spatula, fold two-thirds of whipped cream into cream cheese mixture. Set remaining whipped cream aside for topping.

- Cut konnyaku jelly into cubes and mix well with cream cheese mixture. Pour over prepared base and refrigerate for 1–2 hours or until cake is set.

- To unmould cake, run a small knife around the side of pan. Release clip and lift cake out of ring. Insert a palette knife under the base of cake and lift cake onto a serving plate.

- Garnish with lychees and whipped cream. Serve chilled.

Yoghurt Jelly Strawberry Cheesecake

Makes one 23-cm round cake

DIGESTIVE BISCUIT BASE

Digestive biscuits *180 g, finely crushed*

Unsalted butter *125 g, melted*

FILLING

Gelatine powder *2 Tbsp*

Water *1 Tbsp*

Hot water *3 Tbsp*

Orange juice *150 ml*

Castor sugar *5 Tbsp*

Cream cheese *300 g, at room temperature*

Plain yoghurt *60 g*

Vanilla extract *2 tsp*

Strawberry purée *150 g*

TOPPING

Water *250 ml*

Strawberry jelly crystals *90 g*

Cold water *250 ml*

GARNISHING

Whole strawberries *as needed, halved*

Icing sugar *as needed*

- Grease a 23-cm round springform pan.

- Prepare base. In a mixing bowl, combine digestive biscuits and melted butter. Mix well. Press mixture into the base of prepared springform pan, then freeze until ready to use.

- Prepare filling. In a small bowl, mix gelatine powder with 1 Tbsp water and set aside for 5 minutes. Add 3 Tbsp hot water and stir until gelatine is completely dissolved. Set aside.

- Place orange juice and sugar in a heavy-based saucepan and stir over medium heat until sugar dissolves. Remove from heat and stir in gelatine mixture. Set aside to cool.

- Using an electric mixer with a paddle attachment, beat cream cheese and yoghurt at medium speed until smooth. Add orange-gelatine mixture and beat to combine. Add vanilla extract and strawberry purée. Mix well.

- Pour filling over prepared base and refrigerate for 1–2 hours until firm.

- Prepare topping. In a heavy-based saucepan, bring 250 ml water to the boil over medium heat. Add jelly crystals and stir until dissolved. Remove from heat and add 250 ml cold water. Set aside to cool for 10 minutes.

- Spoon cooled topping onto chilled cake and refrigerate overnight.

- To unmould cake, run a small knife around the side of pan. Release clip and lift cake out of ring. Insert a palette knife under the base of cake and lift cake onto a serving plate.

- Garnish with strawberries and dust with icing sugar. Serve chilled.

Coconut Cream Cheesecake

Makes one 23-cm square cake

Coconut sponge cake base *1 quantity (page 66)*

FILLING

Gelatine powder *1¹/₄ Tbsp*

Water *1 Tbsp*

Hot water *2 Tbsp*

Whipping cream (35% fat) *150 ml, chilled*

60% less fat cream cheese *600 g, at room temperature*

Castor sugar *150 g*

Coconut cream *2 Tbsp*

Vanilla extract *1¹/₂ tsp*

Orange juice *3 tsp*

Desiccated coconut *60 g, toasted + more for garnishing*

Salt *¹/₂ tsp*

- Prepare coconut sponge cake base according to instructions on page 66.

- Prepare filling. In a small bowl, mix gelatine powder with 1 Tbsp water and set aside for 5 minutes. Add 2 Tbsp hot water and stir until gelatine is completely dissolved.

- Using an electric mixer with a whisk attachment and a chilled mixing bowl, whisk whipping cream at medium speed for 1–2 minutes until soft peaks form.

- In another mixing bowl with a paddle attachment, beat cream cheese and sugar at medium speed until smooth. Add coconut cream and beat until combined. Add vanilla extract, orange juice and gelatine mixture and mix well. Add whipped cream and mix thoroughly. Fold in desiccated coconut.

- Spoon filling into a piping bag fitted with a large round tip and pipe straight lines onto coconut sponge cake base until filling is used up. Sprinkle with desiccated coconut and refrigerate overnight.

- To unmould cake, run a small knife around the side of pan. Release clip and lift cake out of ring. Insert a palette knife under the base of cake and lift cake onto a serving plate.

- Garnish as desired and serve chilled.

Peanut Butter Cheesecake

Makes one 23-cm round cake

Digestive biscuit base *1 quantity (page 90)*

FILLING

Gelatine powder *1 Tbsp*

Water *1 Tbsp*

Hot water *2 Tbsp*

80% less fat cream cheese *400 g, at room temperature*

Castor sugar *100 g*

Vanilla extract *2 tsp*

Rose water *1 tsp*

Thickened cream (35% fat) *250 ml*

Creamy peanut butter *340 g*

GARNISHING (OPTIONAL)

Creamy peanut butter *100 g*

Roasted peanuts *as needed*

- Prepare base according to instructions on page 90.

- Prepare filling. In a small bowl, mix gelatine powder with 1 Tbsp water and set aside for 5 minutes. Add 2 Tbsp hot water and stir until gelatine is completely dissolved.

- Using a food processor, process cream cheese, sugar, vanilla extract and rose water until smooth. Add thickened cream and gelatine mixture and process until well mixed. Add peanut butter and incorporate. Pour filling over prepared base and refrigerate overnight.

- To unmould cake, run a small knife around the side of pan. Release clip and lift cake out of ring. Insert a palette knife under the base of cake and lift cake onto a serving plate.

- Garnish with peanut butter and roasted peanuts, if desired. Serve chilled.

Chocolate Peppermint Cheesecake

Makes two 21-cm round cakes

Sponge cake base *1 quantity (page 40)*

Peppermint chocolate *200 g, roughly chopped*

FILLING

Gelatine powder *1¼ Tbsp*

Water *1 Tbsp*

Hot water *2 Tbsp*

Whipping cream (35% fat) *150 ml, chilled*

60% less fat cream cheese *350 g, at room temperature*

Sweetened condensed milk *180 g*

Vanilla extract *2 tsp*

Peppermint essence *½ tsp*

Peppermint chocolate *200 g, melted*

- Grease two 21-cm round disposable aluminium cake pans. Prepare batter for base according to instructions on page 40 and bake base in prepared cake pans.

- Prepare filling. In a small bowl, mix gelatine powder with 1 Tbsp water and set aside for 5 minutes. Add 2 Tbsp hot water and stir until gelatine is completely dissolved.

- Using an electric mixer with a whisk attachment and a chilled mixing bowl, whisk whipping cream at medium speed for 1–2 minutes until soft peaks form.

- In another mixing bowl with a paddle attachment, beat cream cheese at medium speed until smooth. Add condensed milk and mix until incorporated. Add vanilla extract and peppermint essence and mix well. Fold in whipped cream.

- Spoon a portion of filling into a piping bag fitted with a fine round tip. Set aside.

- Add melted peppermint chocolate to remaining filling and stir lightly with chopsticks to create a marbled effect. Pour peppermint filling evenly over prepared cake bases, then pipe plain filling decoratively over it. Refrigerate overnight.

- To unmould cakes, use a pair of scissors to cut open cake pans. Insert a palette knife under the base of cakes and lift onto a serving plate.

- Garnish with chopped peppermint chocolate and serve chilled.

Pistachio Nougat Cheesecake

Makes 9 small cakes

CORNFLAKE BASE

Cornflakes *225 g, finely crushed*

Unsalted butter *125 g, melted*

FILLING

Gelatine powder *1¼ Tbsp*

Water *1 Tbsp*

Hot water *2 Tbsp*

Cream cheese *500 g, at room temperature*

Golden castor sugar *180 g*

Vanilla extract *3 tsp*

Orange juice *2 Tbsp*

Milk *100 ml*

Almond nougat *100 g, finely chopped*

Shelled roasted pistachio nuts *100 g, finely chopped*

GARNISHING

Almond nougat *50 g, roughly chopped*

Shelled roasted pistachio nuts *50 g*

- Prepare base. Have ready 9 waxed paper muffin cups, each 7-cm wide. Mix crushed cornflakes well with melted butter. Press about 1 Tbsp mixture evenly into each muffin cup. Refrigerate for about 30 minutes.

- Preheat oven to 180°C and bake cornflake bases for 15 minutes. Set aside to cool.

- Prepare filling. In a small bowl, mix gelatine powder with 1 Tbsp water and set aside for 5 minutes. Add 2 Tbsp hot water and stir until gelatine is completely dissolved.

- Using a food processor, process cream cheese and sugar until smooth. Add vanilla extract, orange juice and milk and mix until well incorporated. Add gelatine mixture and beat until combined. Fold in chopped nougat and pistachios. Spoon filling over prepared base. Refrigerate overnight.

- Garnish with chopped almond nougat and pistachios and serve chilled.

No-bake Durian Cheesecake

Makes two 20.5-cm square cakes

Sponge cake base *1 quantity (page 40)*

DURIAN PURÉE

Durian flesh *400 g*

Whipping cream (35% fat) *1–3 Tbsp, chilled*

FILLING

Gelatine powder *1¼ Tbsp*

Water *1 Tbsp*

Hot water *2 Tbsp*

Whipping cream (35% fat) *150 ml, chilled*

Cream cheese *400 g, at room temperature*

Light brown sugar *4 Tbsp*

Orange juice *1 Tbsp*

Vanilla extract *1 tsp*

Durian flesh *200 g*

- Prepare base according to instructions on page 40.

- Prepare durian purée. In a food processor, process durian flesh with 1 Tbsp whipping cream until smooth, adding more whipping cream as needed to achieve desired consistency. Chill purée before using.

- Prepare filling. In a small bowl, mix gelatine powder with 1 Tbsp water and set aside for 5 minutes. Add 2 Tbsp hot water and stir until gelatine is completely dissolved.

- Using an electric mixer with a whisk attachment and a chilled mixing bowl, whisk whipping cream at medium speed for 1–2 minutes until soft peaks form.

- In another mixing bowl with a paddle attachment, beat cream cheese and sugar at medium speed until smooth. Add orange juice and vanilla extract and beat at high speed until well mixed. Add gelatine mixture followed by durian purée and beat until well combined. Add whipped cream and mix well. Fold in durian flesh.

- Meanwhile, remove sponge cakes from cake pans. Line each cake pan with a large sheet of plastic wrap, leaving an overhang for easy removal of cake. Replace sponge cakes in cake pans and pour filling evenly over cakes. Refrigerate for at least 6 hours.

- Lift cakes out of cake pans using plastic wrap. Peel off plastic wrap and place cakes on serving plates.

- Garnish as desired and serve chilled.

Chocolate Coffee Cheesecake

Makes one 23-cm round cake

MACADAMIA NUT BASE

Digestive biscuits *220 g*

Macadamia nuts *80 g*

Castor sugar *1 Tbsp*

Unsalted butter *150 g, melted*

FILLING

Gelatine powder *1¼ Tbsp*

Water *1 Tbsp*

Hot water *2 Tbsp*

Whipping cream (35% fat) *200 ml, chilled*

Icing sugar *50 g + 80 g, sifted*

Cream cheese *350 g, at room temperature*

Dark chocolate buttons (70% cocoa) *90 g, melted*

Instant coffee granules *2 Tbsp, dissolved in 1 Tbsp hot water*

Vanilla extract *2 tsp*

Chocolate syrup *100 ml*

- Grease a 23-cm round springform pan. Preheat oven to 180°C.

- Prepare base. Place digestive biscuits, nuts and sugar in a food processor and process until fine. Add melted butter and mix well. Press mixture into base and sides of prepared springform pan and bake for 20 minutes. Leave to cool, then freeze until ready to use.

- Prepare filling. In a small bowl, mix gelatine powder with 1 Tbsp water and set aside for 5 minutes. Add 2 Tbsp hot water and stir until gelatine is completely dissolved.

- Using an electric mixer with a whisk attachment and a chilled mixing bowl, whisk whipping cream with 50 g icing sugar at medium speed for 2–3 minutes until stiff peaks form. Set one-third of whipped cream aside in the refrigerator for garnishing cake. Add gelatine mixture to remaining whipped cream and whisk to combine. Set aside.

- In another mixing bowl with a paddle attachment, beat cream cheese, 80 g icing sugar, melted dark chocolate, coffee, vanilla extract and chocolate syrup at low speed until smooth. Increase to medium speed and add whipped cream-gelatine mixture. Mix well.

- Pour batter over prepared base and refrigerate overnight.

- To unmould cake, run a small knife around the side of pan. Release clip and lift cake out of ring. Insert a palette knife under the base of cake and lift cake onto a serving plate.

- Garnish with reserved whipped cream and chocolate coffee beans, if desired. Serve chilled.

Lemon Raisin Cheesecake with Passion Fruit Topping

Makes one 23-cm round cake

GINGERSNAP COOKIE BASE

Gingersnap cookies *250 g, finely crushed*

Unsalted butter *200 g, melted*

FILLING

Raisins *30 g, chopped*

Lemon *1, grated for zest and squeezed for juice*

Gelatine powder *1¼ Tbsp*

Water *1 Tbsp*

Hot water *2 Tbsp*

Whipping cream (35% fat) *150 ml, chilled*

Cream cheese *350 g, at room temperature*

Sweetened condensed milk *150 ml*

TOPPING

Gelatine powder *2 tsp*

Water *1 Tbsp*

Hot water *2 Tbsp*

Lemon juice *150 ml*

Passion fruit *3, cut and pulp scooped out*

Castor sugar *2 Tbsp*

- Grease a 23-cm round springform pan. Preheat oven to 160°C.

- Prepare base. In a mixing bowl, combine gingersnap cookies and melted butter. Mix well. Press mixture evenly into the base of springform pan and bake for 15 minutes. Leave to cool, then freeze until ready to use.

- Prepare filling. Soak chopped raisins in lemon juice for 30 minutes.

- In a small bowl, mix gelatine powder with 1 Tbsp water and set aside for 5 minutes. Add 2 Tbsp hot water and stir until gelatine is completely dissolved.

- Using an electric mixer with a whisk attachment and a chilled mixing bowl, whisk whipping cream at medium speed for 1–2 minutes until soft peaks form.

- In another mixing bowl with a paddle attachment, combine cream cheese, condensed milk, lemon zest and soaked raisins with lemon juice at medium speed until incorporated. Reduce mixer speed and add gelatine mixture. Beat until well combined. Add whipped cream and mix well.

- Pour filling over prepared base and smoothen top with a spatula dipped first in hot water. Refrigerate overnight.

- Prepare topping. In a small bowl, mix gelatine powder with 1 Tbsp water and stir well. Add 2 Tbsp hot water and stir until gelatine is completely dissolved.

- In a heavy-based saucepan over medium heat, boil lemon juice, passion fruit pulp and sugar until sugar is dissolved. Remove from heat and add gelatine mixture, stirring until gelatine is dissolved. Refrigerate to chill.

- Pouring topping over set cake and refrigerate until set.

- To unmould cake, run a small knife around the side of pan. Release clip and lift cake out of ring. Insert a palette knife under the base of cake and lift cake onto a serving plate.

- Garnish as desired and serve chilled.

White Wine Cheesecake

Makes 20–25 small cakes

WALNUT BISCUIT BASE

Digestive biscuits *200 g, crushed*

Walnuts *80 g*

Unsalted butter *150 g, melted*

FILLING

Gelatine powder *1¹/₄ Tbsp*

Water *1 Tbsp*

Hot water *2 Tbsp*

Whipping cream (35% fat) *150 ml, chilled*

80% less fat cream cheese *340 g, at room temperature*

Castor sugar *150 g*

Rose water *2 tsp*

Vanilla extract *1 tsp*

White wine *4 Tbsp*

Seedless grapes *250 g, peeled and halved*

GARNISHING

Seedless grapes *200 g or more as desired, in small bunches*

White wine *100 ml*

Castor sugar *as needed*

- Prepare 20–25 small round disposable aluminium cups. Preheat oven to 160°C.

- Prepare base. Place digestive biscuits and walnuts in a food processor and process until fine. Transfer mixture to a mixing bowl. Add melted butter and mix well. Spoon 1 Tbsp mixture into each aluminium cup and press evenly into base. Bake for 15 minutes. Leave to cool, then freeze until ready to use.

- Prepare filling. In a small bowl, mix gelatine powder with 1 Tbsp water and set aside for 5 minutes. Add 2 Tbsp hot water and stir until gelatine is completely dissolved. Set aside.

- Using an electric mixer with a whisk attachment and a chilled mixing bowl, whisk whipping cream at medium speed for 1–2 minutes until soft peaks form. Set whipped cream aside.

- In another mixing bowl with a paddle attachment, beat cream cheese and sugar at medium speed until smooth. Add gelatine mixture, rose water, vanilla extract and white wine and mix well. Fold in whipped cream and grapes.

- Spoon filling equally over prepared biscuit bases. Refrigerate overnight.

- Prepare garnishing. Rinse grapes and dip in white wine. Roll in sugar and leave to set on a large plate.

- Garnish cheesecakes with sugar-coated grapes and serve chilled.

Candied Orange Cheesecake

Makes six 12.5-cm round cakes

BUTTER COOKIE BASE

Butter cookies *180 g, finely crushed*

Unsalted butter *150 g, melted*

FILLING

Gelatine powder *1 Tbsp*

Water *2 Tbsp*

Orange juice *140 ml*

60% less fat cream cheese *350 g, at room temperature*

Castor sugar *100 g*

Milk *90 ml*

Finely grated orange zest *1 Tbsp*

TOPPING

Water *250 ml*

Orange-flavoured gelatine powder *90 g*

Cold water *120 ml*

GARNISHING

Water *as needed*

Oranges *2, washed and cut to obtain 12 thin slices*

Cold water *as needed*

Ice cubes *as needed*

Castor sugar *300 g*

- Prepare 6 round disposable aluminium cake pans, each 12.5-cm wide.

- Prepare base. In a mixing bowl, combine butter cookies and melted butter. Mix well. Press mixture evenly into base of cake pans, then freeze until ready to use.

- Prepare filling. In a small bowl, mix gelatine powder with 2 Tbsp water and set aside for 5 minutes. In a heavy-based saucepan over low heat, boil orange juice and let stand for 2 minutes. Add gelatine mixture and heat until gelatine is dissolved. Set aside to cool.

- In a food processor, process cream cheese, sugar, milk and orange zest until smooth. Add orange-gelatine mixture and mix until blended. Pour filling over prepared cookie bases and refrigerate for at least 2 hours or until firm.

- Prepare garnishing. In a small heavy-based saucepan over medium heat, bring some water to the boil. Add sliced oranges and simmer for 1 minute. Drain oranges and place in bowl of cold water filled with ice. Soak for 10 minutes. Using the same pan, bring more water to the boil. Add sugar and heat until sugar is dissolved. Add cooled orange slices and leave to boil for a few minutes. Lower heat and simmer for 1 hour. Drain orange slices and place on a flat tray to cool.

- Prepare topping. In a heavy-based saucepan over medium heat, bring water to the boil. Remove from heat and add orange-flavoured gelatine powder, stirring until dissolved. Add cold water and mix well.

- Remove set cheesecakes from fridge and top with a slice of candied orange. Carefully spoon orange gelatine mixture over cheesecakes. Refrigerate for 1–2 hours until set.

- To unmould cakes, use a pair of scissors to cut open cake pans. Insert a palette knife under the base of cakes and lift onto a serving plate.

- Garnish with remaining candied orange slices and serve chilled.

Blueberry Marshmallow Cheesecake

Makes two 20.5-cm square cakes

Sponge cake base *1 quantity (page 40)*

FILLING

Gelatine powder *1¼ Tbsp*

Water *1 Tbsp*

Hot water *2 Tbsp*

Marshmallows *200 g, cut into small pieces*

Milk *100 ml*

Double cream (48% fat) *200 ml*

Castor sugar *3 Tbsp + 180 g*

Cream cheese *500 g, at room temperature*

Lemon juice *¾ Tbsp*

Finely grated lemon zest *1 tsp*

BLUEBERRY COMPOTE

Blueberries *500 g*

Water *2 Tbsp*

Castor sugar *5 Tbsp*

Lemon *1, grated for zest and squeezed for juice*

- Prepare base according to instructions on page 40.

- Prepare filling. In a small bowl, mix gelatine powder with 1 Tbsp water and set aside for 5 minutes. Add 2 Tbsp hot water and stir until gelatine is completely dissolved. Set aside.

- Place marshmallows and milk in a microwave-safe bowl and heat in the microwave oven on High at 30-second intervals until marshmallows begin to dissolve in the milk. Stir well between intervals and let cool before using. (It does not matter if there are bits of marshmallow left in the mixture.)

- Using an electric mixer with a whisk attachment and a chilled mixing bowl, whisk double cream and 3 Tbsp sugar at medium speed for about 2 minutes until soft peaks form. Set aside.

- In another mixing bowl with a paddle attachment, beat cream cheese and 180 g sugar at medium speed until smooth. Add lemon juice and zest, followed by marshmallow-milk and gelatine mixtures. Mix until incorporated. Add whipped double cream and mix well.

- Pour filling equally over prepared cake bases and refrigerate overnight.

- Prepare blueberry compote. In a heavy-based saucepan over medium heat, combine ingredients and heat gently for 3–4 minutes until sugar is completely dissolved and blueberries are soft. Remove from heat and leave to cool. Refrigerate until needed.

- To unmould cakes, use a pair of scissors to cut open cake pans. Insert a palette knife under the base of cakes and lift onto a serving plate.

- Spoon blueberry compote over cheesecakes before serving. Serve chilled.

Chocolate Banana Cinnamon Cheesecake

Makes twelve 10-cm round cakes

GINGERSNAP COOKIE BASE

Gingersnap cookies *250 g, finely crushed*

Unsalted butter *200 g, melted*

FILLING

Gelatine powder *1¹/₄ Tbsp*

Water *1 Tbsp*

Hot water *2 Tbsp + 1 Tbsp*

Cocoa powder *2 Tbsp*

Chocolate emulco *1 Tbsp*

Whipping cream (35% fat) *125 ml, chilled*

Cream cheese *400 g, at room temperature*

Light brown sugar *125 g*

Lemon juice *1¹/₂ Tbsp*

Vanilla extract *1 tsp*

Cinnamon sugar *¹/₂ tsp*

Very ripe bananas *3, peeled and mashed*

- Prepare twelve 10-cm round disposable aluminium cake pans. Preheat oven to 160°C.

- Prepare base. In a mixing bowl, combine gingersnap cookies and melted butter. Mix well. Divide cookie mixture evenly among cake pans and press evenly into base of pans. Bake for 15 minutes. Leave to cool, then freeze until ready to use.

- Prepare filling. In a small bowl, mix gelatine powder with 1 Tbsp water and set aside for 5 minutes. Add 2 Tbsp hot water and stir until gelatine is completely dissolved. Set aside.

- In another small bowl, mix cocoa powder, chocolate emulco and remaining 1 Tbsp hot water into a runny paste. If paste is thick, add a little water to dilute. Set aside.

- Using an electric mixer with a whisk attachment and a chilled mixing bowl, whisk whipping cream at medium speed for 1–2 minutes until soft peaks form. Set aside.

- In another mixing bowl with a paddle attachment, beat cream cheese and sugar at medium speed until smooth. Add lemon juice, vanilla extract and cinnamon sugar. Mix well. Beat in mashed banana. Add gelatine mixture and whipped cream and mix thoroughly.

- Divide filling into 2 portions. Add chocolate mixture to one and mix well. Leave other portion plain.

- Using separate tablespoons, spoon a dollop of plain batter over prepared cookie bases, followed by a dollop of chocolate batter. Repeat process of layering until filling is used up. Tap pans gently for filling to settle. Refrigerate overnight.

- To unmould cakes, use a pair of scissors to cut open cake pans. Insert a palette knife under the base of cakes and lift onto a serving plate.

- Garnish as desired and serve chilled.

White Chocolate Pomegranate Cheesecake

Makes one 23-cm round cake

Dark cookie base *1 quantity (page 34)*

POMEGRANATE MOLASSES

Pomegranate seeds *250 g*

Water *500 ml*

Castor sugar *7 Tbsp*

Rose water *2 Tbsp*

Lemon juice *2 tsp*

Cinnamon sugar *1 tsp*

FILLING

Gelatine powder *1 Tbsp*

Water *1 Tbsp*

Hot water *2 Tbsp*

Whipping cream (35% fat) *200 ml, chilled*

60% less fat cream cheese *350 g, at room temperature*

Castor sugar *180 g*

Orange juice *1 Tbsp*

White chocolate buttons *120 g, melted*

TOPPING

Water *200 ml*

Raspberry jelly crystals *90 g*

Cold water *80 ml*

Pomegranate seeds *200 g*

- Prepare dark cookie base according to instructions on page 34.

- Prepare pomegranate molasses. Using a food processor, pulse pomegranate seeds and water several times until seeds are broken up. Strain and extract as much juice as possible. In a heavy-based saucepan over medium heat, bring pomegranate juice, castor sugar, rose water, lemon juice and cinnamon sugar to the boil. Stir to dissolve sugar and simmer over low heat for 45–60 minutes until mixture is thick. Set aside until needed.

- Prepare filling. In a small bowl, mix gelatine powder with 1 Tbsp water and set aside for 5 minutes. Add 2 Tbsp hot water and stir until gelatine is completely dissolved. Set aside.

- Using an electric mixer with a whisk attachment and a chilled mixing bowl, whisk whipping cream at medium speed for about 1 minute or until soft peaks form. Set aside.

NOTE:

Pomegranate molasses can be prepared in advance and stored refrigerated for up to 4 weeks.

- In another mixing bowl with a paddle attachment, beat cream cheese and sugar at medium speed until smooth. Add orange juice and 5–6 Tbsp pomegranate molasses and beat again. Add gelatine mixture and mix well. Add whipped cream and incorporate. Add melted white chocolate and mix until well combined.

- Pour filling over prepared base and refrigerate for 2 hours.

- Prepare topping. In a heavy-based saucepan over medium heat, bring water to the boil. Remove from heat and add jelly crystals, stirring until crystals are dissolved. Add cold water and stir to mix.

- Spoon pomegranate seeds evenly over chilled cheesecake, then gently pour jelly mixture over. Refrigerate for at least 6 hours.

- To unmould cake, run a small knife around the side of pan. Release clip and lift cake out of ring. Insert a palette knife under the base of cake and lift cake onto a serving plate.

- Garnish as desired and serve chilled.

Silky Tofu Cheesecake

Makes two 21-cm round cakes

Sponge cake base *1 quantity (page 40)*

FILLING

Silken tofu *500 g*

Gelatine powder *1¼ Tbsp*

Water *1 Tbsp*

Hot water *2 Tbsp*

Whipping cream (35% fat) *200 ml, chilled*

Cream cheese *250 g, at room temperature*

Castor sugar *150 g*

Orange juice *1 Tbsp*

Vanilla extract *2 tsp*

TOPPING

Gelatine powder *1¼ Tbsp*

Water *1 Tbsp + 250 ml*

Hot water *2 Tbsp*

Castor sugar *4 Tbsp*

Canned azuki beans *200 g*

- Grease two 21-cm round disposable aluminium cake pans. Prepare batter for base according to instructions on page 40 and bake base in prepared cake pans.

- Drain tofu for filling. To do this, first place tofu in a microwave-safe bowl and cook in the microwave on High for 20 seconds. Remove tofu and wrap with a clean, dry tea towel. Place on a plate. Place a chopping board over tofu and weigh it down with a heavy object such as a bag of flour or sugar. Leave for 1 hour 30 minutes. Change the towel if it becomes soggy.

- In a small bowl, mix gelatine powder with 1 Tbsp water and set aside for 5 minutes. Add 2 Tbsp hot water and stir until gelatine is completely dissolved. Set aside.

- Using an electric mixer with a whisk attachment and a chilled mixing bowl, whisk whipping cream at medium speed for 1–2 minutes until soft peaks form. Set aside.

- In another mixing bowl with a clean whisk attachment, whisk drained tofu at medium speed until smooth. Add cream cheese and sugar and whisk until creamy. Transfer mixture to a food processor. Add orange juice, vanilla extract and gelatine mixture and process for about 3 minutes until well mixed. Return mixture to the mixing bowl and add whipped cream. Whisk to mix thoroughly.

- Pour filling equally over prepared cake bases and chill for about 2 hours.

- Prepare topping. In a small bowl, mix gelatine powder with 1 Tbsp water and set aside for 5 minutes. Add 2 Tbsp hot water and stir until gelatine is completely dissolved. Set aside.

- In a heavy-based saucepan over medium heat, boil 250 ml water with sugar until sugar dissolves. Add gelatine mixture and mix well. Add red beans and stir to mix. Set aside to cool for 15 minutes, then pour mixture equally into cake pans and refrigerate overnight.

- To unmould cakes, use a pair of scissors to cut open cake pans. Insert a palette knife under the base of cakes and lift onto a serving plate.

- Garnish as desired and serve chilled.

Apricot Yoghurt Cheesecake

Makes one 23-cm round cake

Pecan base *1 quantity (page 86)*

FILLING

Gelatine powder *1¼ Tbsp*

Water *1 Tbsp*

Hot water *2 Tbsp*

60% less fat cream cheese *350 g, at room temperature*

Golden castor sugar *100 g*

Plain yoghurt *100 g*

Orange juice *1 Tbsp*

Vanilla extract *2 tsp*

Canned apricots *480 g; half puréed, half cut into quarters or small cubes*

- Prepare base according to instructions on page 86.

- Prepare filling. In a small bowl, mix gelatine powder with 1 Tbsp water and set aside for 5 minutes. Add 2 Tbsp hot water and stir until gelatine is completely dissolved. Set aside.

- Using an electric mixer with a paddle attachment, beat cream cheese and sugar at medium speed until smooth. Add yoghurt, orange juice and vanilla extract and beat well. Add apricot purée and incorporate. Stir in gelatine mixture until well mixed. Add cut apricots and mix until combined.

- Pour filling over prepared base and refrigerate overnight.

- To unmould cake, run a small knife around the side of pan. Release clip and lift cake out of ring. Insert a palette knife under the base of cake and lift cake onto a serving plate.

- Garnish as desired and serve chilled.

Rainbow Cheesecake

Makes one 23-cm round cake

Red velvet cake base *1 quantity (page 64)*

FILLING

Gelatine powder *1¹/₄ Tbsp*

Water *1 Tbsp*

Hot water *2 Tbsp*

Whipping cream (35% fat) *200 ml, chilled*

Cream cheese *450 g, at room temperature*

Icing sugar *150 g*

Orange juice *2 Tbsp*

Orange essence *2 tsp*

Food colouring (orange, green, purple, pink, blue and yellow) *as needed*

Water *1.25 litres*

Pandan leaves *3, washed and cut into strips*

Castor sugar *150 g*

Plain agar-agar powder *10 g*

- Prepare base according to instructions on page 64.

- Prepare filling. In a small bowl, mix gelatine powder with 1 Tbsp water and set aside for 5 minutes. Add 2 Tbsp hot water and stir until gelatine is completely dissolved. Set aside.

- Using an electric mixer with a whisk attachment and a chilled mixing bowl, whisk whipping cream at medium speed for 1–2 minutes until soft peaks form. Set aside.

- In another mixing bowl with a paddle attachment, beat cream cheese and icing sugar at medium speed until smooth. Add orange juice and orange essence and mix well. Beat in gelatine mixture, then whipped cream.

- Divide filling among 3 bowls. Add orange colouring to one, green colouring to another and purple to the third. Set aside.

- In a heavy-based saucepan over medium heat, bring 1.25 litres water, pandan leaves, sugar and agar-agar powder to the boil, stirring constantly. Remove from heat when mixture starts to bubble. Divide mixture among 3 bowls. Add pink colouring to one, blue colouring to another and yellow colouring to the third. Set aside.

NOTE:
Clear acetate cake collars are available from baking supply shops.

- To assemble, remove red velvet cake base from springform pan and place on a cake board. Wrap cake with a clear acetate cake collar, then pour purple filling onto prepared cake base. Refrigerate for 30 minutes or until set. Use a fork to lightly scratch the surface to enable the next layer to adhere better. Pour pink agar-agar mixture over and chill for 30 minutes or until set. Repeat to alternate the filling and agar-agar layers until ingredients are used up. You will need to use another 2–3 clear acetate cake collars as the cake gets taller.

- Leave to set overnight in the refrigerator.

- To unmould cake, run a small knife around the side of pan. Release clip and lift cake out of ring. Insert a palette knife under the base of cake and lift cake onto a serving plate.

- Garnish as desired and serve chilled.

Raspberry Soy Cheesecake

Makes six 250-ml jars

DIGESTIVE BISCUIT BASE

Digestive biscuits *180 g, finely crushed*

Unsalted butter *125 g, melted*

FILLING

Silky tofu *100 g*

Gelatine powder *¹/₂ Tbsp*

Water *1 tsp*

Hot water *1 Tbsp*

Cream cheese *240 g, at room temperature*

Castor sugar *100 g*

Plain yoghurt *45 g*

Orange juice *1 Tbsp*

Rose water *1 tsp*

Raspberries *100 g (if using frozen, bring to room temperature)*

TOPPING

Whipping cream (35% fat) *80 ml, chilled*

Cocoa powder *2 Tbsp*

Raspberries *6*

- Prepare base. Have ready six 250-ml jars. In a mixing bowl, combine digestive biscuits and melted butter. Mix well. Press 2–3 Tbsp mixture into the base of each jar, then freeze until ready to use.

- Drain tofu for filling. To do this, first place tofu in a microwave-safe bowl and cook in the microwave on High for 20 seconds. Remove tofu and wrap with a clean, dry tea towel. Place on a plate. Place a chopping board over tofu and weigh it down with a heavy object such as a bag of flour or sugar. Leave for 1 hour 30 minutes. Change the towel if it becomes soggy.

- In a small bowl, mix gelatine powder with 1 tsp water and set aside for 5 minutes. Add 1 Tbsp hot water and stir until gelatine is completely dissolved. Set aside.

- Using an electric mixer with a whisk attachment, whisk drained tofu at medium speed until smooth. Add cream cheese and sugar and whisk until creamy. Transfer mixture to a food processor. Add yoghurt, orange juice, rose water and gelatine mixture and process for about 3 minutes until well mixed. Add half the raspberries and process for another minute.

- Place remaining raspberries into prepared jars. Spoon filling over and refrigerate for 2–3 hours.

- Prepare topping. In another mixing bowl with a clean whisk attachment, whisk whipping cream for 1–2 minutes until stiff peaks form. Add cocoa powder and whisk until combined. Spoon cream into a piping bag fitted with a piping tip and pipe into jars.

- Top with raspberries and serve chilled.

Cempedak Cheesecake

Makes one 19-cm round cake

DIGESTIVE BISCUIT BASE

Digestive biscuits *180 g, finely crushed*

Unsalted butter *125 g, melted*

FILLING

Gelatine powder *³/₄ Tbsp*

Water *1 tsp*

Hot water *1 Tbsp*

Whipping cream (35% fat) *80 ml, chilled*

Cream cheese *250 g, at room temperature*

Castor sugar *70 g*

Orange juice *1 Tbsp*

Cempedak *150 g, puréed + 100 g, cut into small cubes*

TOPPING

Cempedak *80 g, puréed + 200 g, shredded*

- Prepare base. Grease a 19-cm round springform pan and set aside. In a mixing bowl, combine digestive biscuits and melted butter. Mix well. Press mixture into base of prepared pan, then freeze until ready to use.

- In a small bowl, mix gelatine powder with 1 tsp water and set aside for 5 minutes. Add 1 Tbsp hot water and stir until gelatine is completely dissolved. Set aside.

- Using an electric mixer with a whisk attachment and a chilled mixing bowl, whisk whipping cream at medium speed for about 1 minute until soft peaks form. Set aside.

- In another mixing bowl with a paddle attachment, beat cream cheese and sugar at medium speed until smooth. Add orange juice and mix well. Add gelatine mixture and mix until incorporated. Add cempedak purée and beat until well combined. Fold in whipped cream.

- Scatter cubed cempedak over prepared base. Pour filling over base and refrigerate for 2 hours.

- Prepare topping. Spoon cempedak purée into a piping bag. Snip off the pointed end and pipe concentric circles on set filling. Using a chopstick, draw lines to create a pattern. Refrigerate overnight.

- To unmould cake, run a small knife around the side of pan. Release clip and lift cake out of ring. Insert a palette knife under the base of cake and lift cake onto a serving plate.

- Top with shredded cempedak and serve chilled.

NOTE:

If cempedak is not available, substitute with jackfruit.

Low Fat Blackberry Cheesecake

Makes one 21-cm square cake

DIGESTIVE BISCUIT BASE

Digestive biscuits *180 g, finely crushed*

Unsalted butter *125 g, melted*

FILLING

Gelatine powder *1¼ Tbsp*

Water *1 Tbsp*

Hot water *2 Tbsp*

80% less fat cream cheese *350 g, at room temperature*

Castor sugar *170 g*

Ricotta cheese *300 g*

Vanilla extract *2 tsp*

Finely grated lemon zest *2 tsp*

Lemon juice *1 Tbsp*

Blackberries (fresh or frozen) *150 g*

BLACKBERRY COMPOTE

Blackberries (fresh or frozen) *350 g*

Castor sugar *4 Tbsp*

Finely grated lemon zest *1 tsp*

Lemon juice *1 Tbsp*

Strawberry jelly crystals *2 Tbsp*

- Prepare base. Line a 21-cm square cake pan with aluminium foil, leaving an overhang for easy removal of cake. In a mixing bowl, combine digestive biscuits and melted butter. Mix well. Press mixture into base of prepared pan, then freeze until ready to use.

- Prepare filling. In a small bowl, mix gelatine powder with 1 Tbsp water and set aside for 5 minutes. Add 2 Tbsp hot water and stir until gelatine is completely dissolved. Set aside.

- Using an electric mixer with a paddle attachment, beat cream cheese and sugar at medium speed until smooth. Add ricotta cheese and beat until combined. Add vanilla extract, lemon zest and juice and beat for 1 minute. Add gelatine mixture and mix well.

- Scatter blackberries over prepared base and pour filling over base. Refrigerate overnight.

- Prepare topping. In a heavy-based saucepan over medium heat, combine all topping ingredients and cook, stirring, until sugar and jelly crystals are dissolved. Remove from heat and set aside to cool.

- Lift cake out of pan using aluminium foil and place on a flat serving plate. Insert a palette knife under the base of cake and lift cake. Peel off aluminium foil and replace cake on serving plate.

- Slice cake and top with blackberry compote. Serve chilled.

Kiwi Cheesecake

Makes two 20.5-cm square cakes

Sponge cake base *1 quantity (page 40)*

FILLING
Gelatine powder *1$\frac{1}{4}$ Tbsp*
Water *1 Tbsp*
Hot water *2 Tbsp*

Cream cheese *250 g, at room temperature*
Icing sugar *100 g, sifted*
Vanilla extract *1$\frac{1}{2}$ tsp*
Orange juice *1 Tbsp*
Whipping cream (35% fat) *100 ml, chilled*
Kiwi fruit *2, peeled and cut into cubes*

* Grease two 20.5-cm square disposable aluminium cake pans and prepare base according to instructions on page 40.

* Prepare filling. In a small bowl, mix gelatine powder with 1 Tbsp water and set aside for 5 minutes. Add 2 Tbsp hot water and stir until gelatine is completely dissolved. Set aside.

* Using an electric mixer with a whisk attachment and a chilled mixing bowl, whisk whipping cream at medium speed until soft peaks form. Set aside.

* In another mixing bowl with a paddle attachment, beat cream cheese and icing sugar until smooth. Add vanilla extract and orange juice and beat for 30 seconds. Add gelatine mixture and mix well. Add whipped cream and beat well. Fold in cubed kiwi fruit.

* Pour filling evenly over prepared cake bases and refrigerate overnight.

* To unmould cakes, use a pair of scissors to cut open cake pans. Insert a palette knife under the base of cakes and lift onto a serving plate.

* Garnish as desired and serve chilled.

Matcha Cheesecake

Makes one 23-cm round cake

Macadamia nut base *1 quantity (page 48)*

FILLING

Gelatine powder *1 Tbsp*

Water *1 Tbsp*

Hot water *2 Tbsp*

Whipping cream (35% fat) *80 ml + 250 ml, chilled*

Cream cheese *450 g, at room temperature*

Castor sugar *120 g*

Salt *a pinch*

Vanilla extract *1 tsp*

Rose water *1 tsp*

Maple syrup *3 Tbsp*

Matcha (green tea) powder *2 Tbsp + more for decorating cake*

- Prepare base according to instructions on page 48.

- Prepare filling. In a small bowl, mix gelatine powder with 1 Tbsp water and set aside for 5 minutes. Add 2 Tbsp hot water and stir until gelatine is completely dissolved. Set aside.

- In a heavy-based saucepan over low heat, heat 80 ml whipping cream and stir in matcha powder. Mix well. Leave to cool.

- Using an electric mixer with a whisk attachment and a chilled mixing bowl, whisk 250 ml whipping cream at medium speed for about 1 minute until soft peaks form. Set aside.

NOTE:

This cake goes well with an orange-ginger drink. To prepare this drink, place 2 slices of ginger and 1 Tbsp grated orange zest in a teapot. Add 450 ml boiling water and steep for 30 minutes. Strain. Reheat to serve warm.

- In another mixing bowl with a paddle attachment, beat cream cheese, sugar and salt until smooth. Add vanilla extract, rose water and maple syrup and beat for 1 minute. Add gelatine mixture and mix well. Add matcha whipping cream mixture and whipped cream and beat until combined.

- Pour filling over prepared base. Using a spatula dipped first in warm water, spread filling out evenly. Refrigerate overnight.

- To unmould cake, run a small knife around the side of pan. Release clip and lift cake out of ring. Insert a palette knife under the base of cake and lift cake onto a serving plate.

- Dust cake with matcha powder and serve chilled.

Black Sesame Cheesecake

Makes one 23-cm round cake

Dark cookie base *1 quantity (page 34)*

FILLING

Gelatine powder *1¹/₄ Tbsp*

Water *1 Tbsp*

Hot water *2 Tbsp*

Whipping cream (35% fat) *240 ml, chilled*

Cream cheese *450 g, at room temperature*

Milk *60 ml*

Vanilla extract *2 tsp*

Orange juice *1 Tbsp*

Icing sugar *100 g*

Black sesame paste *180 g*

Black sesame seeds *2 Tbsp, roasted + more for garnishing*

- Prepare dark cookie base according to instructions on page 34.

- Prepare filling. In a small bowl, mix gelatine powder with 1 Tbsp water and set aside for 5 minutes. Add 2 Tbsp hot water and stir until gelatine is completely dissolved. Set aside.

- Using an electric mixer with a whisk attachment, whisk whipping cream at medium speed for 1 minute until soft peaks form. Set aside.

- Using a food processor, process cream cheese, milk, vanilla extract, orange juice and icing sugar until smooth. Add gelatine mixture and process for about 1 minute until well mixed. Add whipped cream and mix well.

- Pour two-thirds of filling into a mixing bowl and set aside. Add black sesame paste and sesame seeds to remaining filling in food processor and process until smooth.

- Pour half the plain filling over prepared base and top with a few scoops of sesame filling. Cover with the remaining plain filling and repeat to top with another few scoops of sesame filling. Using a chopstick or skewer, swirl filling to create a marbled effect.

- Spoon remaining sesame filling into a piping bag fitted with a piping tip and pipe to garnish cake. Sprinkle with black sesame seeds and refrigerate overnight.

- To unmould cake, run a small knife around the side of pan. Release clip and lift cake out of ring. Insert a palette knife under the base of cake and lift cake onto a serving plate.

- Serve chilled.

Avocado Gula Melaka Cheesecake

Makes two 16-cm round cakes

DIGESTIVE BISCUIT BASE
Digestive biscuits *180 g, finely crushed*
Unsalted butter *125 g, melted*

FILLING
Gelatine powder *1 Tbsp*
Water *1 Tbsp*
Hot water *2 Tbsp*
Milk *150 ml*

Palm sugar (*gula melaka*) *180 g*
Cream cheese *450 g, at room temperature*
Orange juice *2 Tbsp*
Vanilla extract *2 tsp*

AVOCADO CREAM
Whipping cream (35% fat) *150 ml, chilled*
Avocado *2, peeled and puréed*

- Prepare base. Line two 16-cm round cake pans with aluminium foil, leaving an overhang for easy removal of cake. Grease well. In a mixing bowl, combine digestive biscuits and melted butter. Mix well. Press mixture into base of prepared pan, then freeze until ready to use.

- Prepare filling. In a small bowl, mix gelatine powder with 1 Tbsp water and set aside for 5 minutes. Add 2 Tbsp hot water and stir until gelatine is completely dissolved. Set aside.

- In a heavy-based saucepan over medium heat, heat milk and palm sugar, stirring until sugar is dissolved. Strain and measure out 100 ml milk mixture. Set aside.

- Using an electric mixer with a paddle attachment, beat cream cheese until smooth. Add milk mixture and beat for 1 minute. Add gelatine mixture, orange juice and vanilla extract and mix to incorporate.

- Pour filling equally over prepared biscuit bases and refrigerate overnight.

- Prepare avocado cream. In another mixing bowl with a whisk attachment, whisk whipping cream at medium speed for about 1 minute until soft peaks form. Add avocado purée and mix well.

- Spoon avocado cream into a piping bag fitted with a piping tip and pipe decoratively over cake.

- Lift cake out of pan using aluminium foil and place on a flat serving plate. Insert a palette knife under the base of cake and lift cake. Peel off aluminium foil and replace cake on serving plate.

- Garnish as desired and serve chilled.